Hospice at Hom Carlisle and Nor Lakeland

Hospice at Home provides a specially trained palliative care nursing service for people with a terminal illness who prefer to remain in their own home with all that is loved and familiar about them, and gives support and help to those caring for them.

- The service provides nursing care and support in the patient's home.

- The service is free of all charges to the patient and their carers.

- The service applies to terminally ill patients, of any age, suffering from any life threatening illness, who choose to die in their own home.

- As far as possible the care is tailored to patient and carer needs.

- We have no building to maintain: so more of the money donated goes directly to the nursing service and bereavement support.

- The service covers the whole of rural North and East Cumbria and the City of Carlisle - approximately 1,500 square miles with a population of 188,000.

Hospice at Home Carlisle and North Lakeland aims to make staying at home a realistic choice while ensuring the best quality of life, with proper care, support, dignity, comfort and humour for the patient, their family and carers and hopes ultimately to relieve some of the pain of bereavement.

Hospice at Home
Carlisle and North Lakeland
The Fundraising Office, Gilwilly Industrial Estate
Penrith, Cumbria, CA11 9BL
Tel: 01768 210719
www.hospiceathome.co.uk

Acknowledgements

Recipes with a Citrus Twist is the result of a concerted team effort and we are confident that it will prove to be a wonderful asset to you in your kitchen at home.

The impetus for the book came from Jane Hasell-McCosh, following the success of The World's First Marmalade Festival in 2007 - held at the family's historic home Dalemain, near Penrith.

Special thanks to the Marmalade Festival committee members who helped to put the book together on behalf of Hospice at Home Carlisle & North Lakeland: Caroline Addison, Annie Binny, Jane Callaghan, Jenny Harris, Juliet Westoll and especially Ivan Day and Annette Gibbons. Thanks also to Sheila Thompson (charity director) and Katarzyna Gajewska (Office Manager) for their help.

The committee is particularly grateful to Carrs Breadmaker for their wonderful support for Hospice at Home Carlisle & North Lakeland by sponsoring *Recipes with a Citrus Twist* and parent company, Carr's Milling Industries plc, for its generous sponsorship of The World's Original Marmalade Festival in 2008.

We would like to thank Mandy Norwood from *Cumbria Life* magazine for kindly overseeing this project and Alison Turnbull and Julie Hutchinson for the book's excellent design.

Our grateful thanks go to Anne-Marie McMillan for her meticulous tying up of the recipes and Janet Arnison for her kindness in helping to proof read the book.

A massive amount of work also went into the production of the photography and thanks go to the wonderful Cumbrian cooks Sara Ecroyd and Yvonne Marples, together with Annie Binny, Jane Callaghan, Diane Wilson, and also to Brenda Dowding of Gardenalia who went to so much trouble with the presentation of the food.

Thanks to *Cumbria Life* photographers Paula Paisley, Louise Porter, Stewart Blair and Stuart Walker for their fantastic pictures.

Our final thanks must, of course, go to everyone who has contributed a recipe to the book - sales of which will help to support the incredibly important service provided by Hospice at Home Carlisle & North Lakeland.

Some useful Conversions

WEIGHTS	LIQUID MEASURES
1 ounce - 25g	1 teaspoon - 5ml
4 ounces - 125g	1 tablespoon - 15ml
8 ounces - 225g	1/4 pint (5floz) - 150ml
12 ounces - 350g	1/2 pint (10floz) - 300ml
16 ounces - 450g	1 pint (20floz) - 600ml

Contents

A selection of early marmalades

A Short History of Marmalade

in five recipes By Ivan Day, food historian www.historicfood.com

Chardequince

As early as the 15th century a sweet quince preserve called marmalada was being imported into these islands from southern Europe. This luxury item came mainly from Portugal, where the name for quince was marmelo. However, at this time there was also an excellent native English quince marmalade, which was called chardequince. This sweet, spicy confection was really the mother of all British marmalades and no book on the subject would be complete without a recipe for it. Chardequince is not only easy to make, but is really delicious. The following recipe is adapted from a Plantaganet cookery manuscript in the British Library. In Middle-English, the word char meant 'flesh', so chardequince was literally 'flesh of quinces'. Our medieval ancestors also made chardewardoun from pears, chardecrabbe from crabapples and chardedate from dates.

Peeled, cored and chopped up quince flesh 1lb, red wine 10fl oz, honey 14oz
1 stick of cinnamon, 1 teaspoon of powdered ginger

You will need two large quinces or four smallish ones to yield 16oz of flesh. Peel and core the fruit and chop it into small pieces. Put it into a saucepan and cover with the wine. Cover the saucepan and bring to the boil. Turn the heat down and let the fruit simmer gently until it is soft. This should take about 35 minutes, but it will depend on the quality of your quinces. Drain the wine off and use it for something else – (I add some sugar and make it into a syrup for pouring over vanilla ice cream – delicious!). It is the cooked quince flesh that you need. Turn the quince flesh into puree in a food processor, or rub through a sieve and transfer to a wide bottomed preserving pan. Add the honey and cinnamon stick and gently cook until it turns to a thick liquid, continuously stirring with a wooden spoon. When it comes to the boil, turn the heat down and never stop stirring. At first the mixture will resemble jam, but after a while it will start to thicken. It is very important to keep it constantly moving around the pan with the spoon. If you stop it could burn. You will need to do this for about 25 to 30 minutes. After this time test a small spoonful on a plate. If after a few minutes it sets into a firm, thick paste rather like unset toffee, it is ready and you must take it off the heat. Stir in the ginger thoroughly. The setting time depends on the pectin level in the quinces. It could take longer than 30 minutes. Spoon the hot paste onto a lightly oiled sheet of baking parchment and using a wet palette knife smooth it out into block about half an inch thick. The next day it should have set into a fairly solid paste. You can cut it up into squares which you can roll in caster sugar. If you want a real period effect you can print patterns on it with wet wooden butter prints and even gild it with edible gold leaf. This honey-flavoured, cornelian coloured confection is delicious served with cheese.

Red Quince Marmalade

and cotoniac Here are two recipes for the price of one.

By the 16th century, the English name chardequince had been completely replaced by the Portuguese marmalade, honey was substituted with sugar and the spices were usually omitted. Recipes for both red and white quince marmalades are among the most common preserves included in late Tudor and early Stuart cookery texts. To make the marmalade red, the quinces were usually cooked longer, or the juice of barberries, bullaces or sloes was added. These marmalades were still thick pastes, and bore no resemblance to our modern jam-like marmalade made from oranges. They were thought to be an excellent medicine for digestion, which led them to be eaten at the end of the meal. The waste materials - peel, cores and pips – produced by making this marmalade were used to produce an extraordinary thick quince jelly called cotoniac or quiddany.

To make red quince marmalade (adapted from a recipe from the time of James I).
6 medium sized quinces, 2 pints of water

Cover the quinces with the water and poach them gently for about an hour in a covered saucepan. They should be very soft when cooked. Let them cool and pull off the peel. Remove the cores, pips and any woody flesh adjacent to the core, but save all this waste material and the skins if you want to make the cotoniac in the next recipe.

Add a cup of the strained water in which you poached the quinces and turn them into a smooth puree in a liquidiser. Turn this out into a broad bottomed preserving pan and cook it gently over a low heat, stirring continuously with a wooden spoon. After about twenty minutes or more, the puree will start to thicken. It is essential to keep stirring or it may burn. At this stage it will also start to change to pinkish or pale brick red colour. When it has reduced by about a half in volume it is time to weigh the puree.

This is easily done if you know the weight of your preserving pan in advance. Allow the pan to cool until you can safely put it on your scales. Add to it an equal weight of sugar. Return the pan to the heat. With the addition of the sugar it will become more liquid. Cook it gently, stirring continuously. After another twenty minutes it will start to thicken and will reduce in volume. It will also change to a colour which our ancestors called 'a beautiful orient red'. Test a small quantity on a plate. After a few minutes this should set into a paste, which you should be able to roll into a ball between your fingers. If it is more like a sticky jam it needs cooking a little longer.

Pour the paste onto a lightly oiled sheet or baking parchment. Flatten it with a wet palette knife into a block about half an inch thick and leave to set. The next day it should have set into a thick paste. This was traditionally stored in round wooden boxes rather like the ones that are used for Camembert cheese or Turkish Delight. It can also be rolled out into long thin 'sausages' and tied into knots.

Cotoniac or Quidanny

In its heyday, this was considered to be a form of quince marmalade, but is really a thickened quince jelly which has the most wonderful Turkish Delight-like texture and a glass-like reflective surface. It was stored in round boxes.

Quince cores, skins, pips left over from previous recipe,
cooking water from previous recipe, 5fl oz of extra water

If you have made the quince marmalade from the previous recipe, put the cores, skins and pips of the quinces back into the water you used to originally boil the whole fruit. Return a cup of fresh water to the saucepan to make up for the one you removed earlier. Cook very gently with the lid on for about 40 minutes. Strain the liquid. You can now throw all the waste cores etc. away. Put the liquid back into the saucepan and simmer it very slowly without a lid to reduce it to half a pint. To half a pint of the juice add 8 ozs of white granulated sugar. Transfer to a wide preserving pan and cook gently for about twenty minutes or until it starts to become quite thick and glutinous in the pan. Pour into a round wooden box – a recycled Turkish Delight box is ideal. Store with the lid on like chardequince and quince marmalade.

Elizabeth Rainbow's
Red Quince Marmalade

Elizabeth Rainbow, wife of the Bishop of Carlisle, lived at Dalemain and compiled her own recipe book in the closing decades of the 17th century. The book has survived and is one of the great historic treasures of Dalemain. By Elizabeth's lifetime, marmalade had become a general term for all kinds of fruit preserves, other than those made from quinces or oranges. Marmalades were made from cherries, apricots and even orange flowers. They were also becoming more like jellies and jams, rather than the thick pastes of the earlier periods. This recipe is in Elizabeth's own words.

To make red marmalade of quinces

Take a pound of sugar & beat it very fine, then take your quinces (being raw) & pare them, & cut them in small thin slices, but not too near the core, as you cut them cover them up in your sugar, & when you have 2 lb. of your sugar, & quince together, then put all together into a skillet with almost a wine pint of fair water, & set it to boil an indifferent pace; & when your quince is tender, & turned red, take it out of the syrup into a silver, or earthen basin, & break it with a spoon very small, & let the syrup boil the whilst, then put it into the syrup again; & when your marmalade is boiled thick enough, & that it comes clean from the bottom of the skillet, take it off the fire, & put it into boxes, or glasses. Cover not your marmalade at all in the boiling; or if you do, not until it be turned tawny.

Gervase Markham's
Marmalade of Oranges

Marmalade started to be made with oranges in the late Tudor period. One of the earliest recipes was included in The English Housewife, a cookery book written by Gervase Markham and published in 1615. The Markham family have had strong connections with Cumbria for nearly 200 years and live in the village of Morland. Like its close relative the quince marmalade, this very early orange marmalade is a thick paste. Here is Markham's recipe in its original Shakespearian English:

To make an excellent Marmalade of Oranges

Take the Oranges and with a knife pare off as thin as is possible the uppermost rind of the Orange; yet in such sort, as by no means you alter the colour of the Orange; then steep them in faire water, changing the water twice a day till you find no bitterness of taste therein; then take them forth, and first boyl them in faire running water, and when they are soft, remove them into rose-water, and boyl them therein till they break; then to every pound of the pulpe, put a pound of refined Sugar, and so having masht and stirring them all well together, straine it through very fair strainers into boxes, and so use it as you shall see occasion.

Marmalades, Curds, Preserves & Relishes

Lemon Curd and Seville Orange Curd (page 13)

Seville Orange Curd

2 large whole eggs plus 2
large egg yolks
4oz/100g butter
4oz/100g caster sugar
grated rind and juice of 2
Seville oranges
Makes approx 12oz/350g

LADY CLAIRE MACDONALD,
AWARD-WINNING COOK AND
FOOD WRITER. KINLOCH
LODGE, ISLE OF SKYE

In a jug beat together the 2 whole eggs and the 2 yolks, then sieve them into a bowl.

Cut up the butter into the bowl, and add the sugar and orange rinds and juice.

Put the bowl over a saucepan of gently simmering water, and stir occasionally (there's no need to stir continuously) until the curd is really thick.

Take the bowl off the heat, and spoon the curd into jars or a bowl. Leave to cool. Store in the refrigerator.

Orange or lemon curd is wonderfully useful folded into whipped cream as a filling for meringues or light sponge cakes, quite apart from spreading on warm brown toast or hot scones! I've tried making curd with sweet oranges, but it lacks the necessary sharp tang and isn't very pleasant at all. When it's made with Seville oranges, on the other hand, you get the full orange flavour with the citrus sharpness, quite delicious. A jar of orange or lemon curd makes a good little present too!

Lemon Curd

720g caster sugar
360g butter, melted
8 eggs
4 egg yolks
4 lemons, zest and juice

JOHN BADLEY,
EXECUTIVE HEAD CHEF,
MACDONALD LEEMING HOUSE,
WATERMILLOCK

Mix and slowly bring to simmer.

tip.....

Delicious spread on Carrs Breadmaker's Orange & Poppy Seed Rolls (page 90) for a teatime treat.

Preserving Orange, Lemon and other Citrus Peels

1 kg granulated white sugar
lemon, orange or other citrus
peels cut into quarters
1 litre of water

tip.....

*Use only the peels of unwaxed
or genuine organic fruit.*

IVAN DAY, FOOD HISTORIAN
www.historicfood.com

To make stock syrup:

For each type of fruit, heat 1 litre of water until it boils. Take it off the heat and stir into it 1kg of white granulated sugar. Keep stirring until every crystal of sugar has dissolved. This amount of syrup will be enough to preserve about 1kg of citrus peels.

To preserve the peels:

Cook the peels by gently boiling them in some clean water until they feel quite soft. This usually takes about 45 minutes, but can vary. Take them out of the water and drain them. Put your syrup back on the heat and bring it to the boil. When it comes to the boil gently cook the peels in the syrup for 7 minutes. The syrup should just gently simmer while this is being done. After 7 minutes pour the syrup and peels into a ceramic bowl and when cool, cover to protect from insects and dust. Let the fruit stay in the syrup for 24 hours. After 24 hours sieve the syrup into a saucepan but leave the fruit in the ceramic bowl. Boil the syrup for 5 minutes and then pour over the fruit. Do not be tempted to cook the peels in the syrup now because it will make them tough. Leave the fruit in the syrup for 24 hours and repeat this procedure for 10 more days. The syrup will eventually get much thicker.

After 12 days you can leave the fruit in the syrup and keep them in well-sealed jars as you would jam. Keep the jar in the fridge. I prefer to keep my fruit in the syrup until I use it rather than candying it, as it stays succulent and does not become tough and dry.

To candy the peels:

Remove them from the syrup. Wash off all traces of syrup under some hot water. Put them on a metal cake rack over a tin to catch any drips and leave them in a warm dry place. For candied fruit a lot of modern recipes use a proportion of glucose syrup in the sugar syrup to help keep them moist but this destroys the flavour of the fruit.

Marmalade

1½lb/700g Seville oranges
1½lb/700g other citrus fruit or perhaps a grapefruit, a sweet orange and the balance of weight made up with good tasting tangerines or clementines
6lb/2.75kg granulated or preserving sugar

makes 11 – 12lb

Put the fruit in a large saucepan or ham pan with 4 pints of water and simmer gently for about 6 hours.

Remove the fruit from the water in the pan and cut each orange, tangerine or grapefruit in half.

Scoop out all the pips into a small saucepan, cover with ½ pint water and simmer for 10 minutes.

Leave to cool, then strain this liquid into the jam pan with the water the fruit was cooked in.

While the pips are simmering, cut up the fruit (I put mine in a food processor).

Put the cut-up fruit back in the water in the jam pan.

Add the sugar and cook on a low heat, stirring occasionally until the sugar has completely dissolved. Then boil furiously, and after 10 minutes pull the pan off the heat to test whether the marmalade is setting. Do this by dripping some of the hot marmalade on to a cold saucer.

Leave it for a few minutes and if, when you push the surface of the sample with the top of your finger, the skin on top of the marmalade wrinkles you have a set.

If it is still runny put the jam pan back on the heat, boil vigorously for a further 5 minutes and test again. Always remember to pull the pan off the heat while testing for a set otherwise it may go too far.

Pot when still hot into warmed jars and cover with a circle of waxed paper. Seal completely with cellophane and rubber bands when quite cold.

LADY CLAIRE MACDONALD, AWARD-WINNING COOK AND FOOD WRITER. KINLOCH LODGE, ISLE OF SKYE
www.claire-macdonald.com

tip.....

Spread on fresh toast made from Carrs Breadmaker's Stilton & Marmalade Bread (page 89).

Onion and Orange Marmalade Relish

1lb/500g peeled and finely sliced onions
2 tbsp olive oil
sprig fresh rosemary
rind of 1 orange
2 tbsp soft brown sugar
seasoning to taste
5 fl oz/150ml white wine
3 tbsp white wine vinegar
juice of 1 orange
1 tbsp Seville orange marmalade

Heat the oil in a saucepan, add the onions, the sprig of rosemary and grated orange rind. Fry for a few minutes until beginning to soften and brown slightly.
Add the brown sugar, white wine, wine vinegar and the orange juice; allow to simmer but then turn down the heat.
Cook on a low heat for up to 1 hour or until almost all of the liquid has cooked away and the onions are very tender.
Remove from the heat and stir in the Seville orange marmalade. Store in a sterile screw top jar.

tip.....

This savoury marmalade is delicious with all cold meats, cheeses and kipper pate.

JOAN GATE AND MARGARET BROUGH,
FOOD AND COMPANY,
HESKET NEWMARKET
www.foodandcompany.co.uk

Beetroot and Orange Relish

450g/1lb fresh beetroot
450g/1lb onions, chopped
2 oranges, grated rind and juice
1 tsp salt, 6 star anise
1 tsp fennel seeds
350g/¾lb sugar
570ml/1 pint pickling vinegar

To cook the beetroot put into a large pan and cover with cold water. Bring to the boil and simmer until tender. Drain, peel and roughly chop into small pieces.
Put all the other ingredients into a large pan and bring slowly to the boil. Simmer until a good consistency is reached. Test for seasoning. Pour into sterilised jars.

NICK MARTIN,
www.nickofthyme.co.uk

Salted Lemons

10 unwaxed lemons
125g coarse sea salt
1 bay leaf
10 coriander seeds
1 large jar

GAVIN IRVING, HEAD CHEF,
CROSBY LODGE HOTEL

Slice each lemon in half length ways, then slice each half, half way through width ways.
Take a good pinch of salt and rub gently into the lemons.
Pack 5 lemons in the jar pressing firm to release some of the juice. Add bay leaf and half the salt that is left.
Repeat with the other 5 lemons and add remainder of the salt and coriander seeds.
If lemon juice does not cover the lemons top up with a good olive oil.
Seal the jar and leave for at least 1 month.
Delicious served with grilled fish, chicken or lamb.

Salads
& Starters

Lemon and Fennel Salad (page 21)

Baked Lemons

filled with Morecambe Bay Shrimps and Cumberland Dairy Keldthwaite Gold Cheese

2 medium sized lemons
2 pots of Morecambe Bay brown shrimps in butter
2oz/50g of softened Cumberland Dairy Keldthwaite Gold Cheese, skin removed
a small sprig of fresh coriander and parsley
fresh ground black pepper

serves 4

tip.....

Recipe can be doubled or trebled for a party food.

Cut the lemons in half widthways.

Carefully cut a small slice from the ends so the lemon halves sit level. Take a knife and carefully cut around the inside rim and remove the pulp. Then use a teaspoon to carefully scrape out pulp from the inside of the lemon cup.

Place the shrimps in a bowl, add the chopped coriander and parsley. Season with the pepper and mix well.

Use a spoon to fill the lemon cups with the shrimps and pack them in well.

Neatly spread the cheese on top.

Place the lemons on to a baking dish and place in a hot oven at 180C/gas mark 7 for ten minutes until the cheese has browned. Remove from the oven and leave for five minutes before tucking in with crusty bread.

NICK MARTIN,
www.nickofthyme.co.uk

Lemon and Fennel Salad

1 top quality lemon
1 large head of fennel

serves 4

tip.....

Serve with roast lamb or pork chops and roast potatoes and equally delicious with Carrs Breadmaker's Pissaladière (page 91).

Slice the lemon lengthways in half and then cut each half into very, very thin slices, skin and all.

Cut the fresh fennel into slightly thicker slices that are small enough to be a mouthful.

Mix them in a bowl with this dressing:
$\frac{1}{2}$ small pot of single cream
small squeeze of lemon juice
$\frac{1}{2}$ tsp of caster sugar
salt to taste.

NICHOLAS LANDER, FOOD WRITER FOR FINANCIAL TIMES, HUSBAND OF JANCIS ROBINSON, WINE CORRESPONDENT AND BROADCASTER. PATRON - HOSPICE AT HOME CARLISLE AND NORTH LAKELAND

Citrus Marinated Prawns

500g prawns (defrosted)
orange
lemon
lime
radicchio lettuce
cracked black pepper
fresh coriander

serves 4

JOANNE KERSWELL,
SEVEN BAR AND RESTAURANT,
COCKERMOUTH

Zest and juice lemon, orange and lime, keeping zest and juice separate. Place prawns in a dish and pour on citrus juice, a pinch of cracked black pepper and a small bunch of chopped coriander. Chill for 15/20 minutes.

Wash radicchio leaves and place 1 or 2 leaves in the centre of a plate to create a bowl. Drain prawns and put around 3 tablespoons of prawns in the centre of the leaves and top with mixed zest, coriander leaves and serve.

Moroccan Carrot and Orange Salad

450g/1lb carrots, peeled and coarsely grated
2 oranges, peeled, white pith removed and cut crossways into 1cm/$\frac{1}{2}$in slices, then into small segments
2 tbsp orange juice
1 tbsp lemon juice
2 tbsp extra virgin olive oil
sea salt and freshly ground black pepper
$\frac{1}{2}$ tsp ground cumin
$\frac{1}{2}$ tsp ground cinnamon
1 tsp icing sugar
handful of fresh coriander or mint leaves

serves 4

Combine the orange juice, lemon juice, olive oil, sea salt, pepper, cumin, cinnamon and icing sugar in a bowl and whisk. Add the grated carrot, orange segments and coriander or mint and lightly toss.

 tip.....

You can also serve this with a couple of bunches of watercress. In summer strew some sliced summer radishes over the top for extra crunch.

NICK MARTIN,
www.nickofthyme.co.uk

Orange Dressing

5 oranges, juiced (zest of 2)
3 limes, juiced (zest of 2)
2oz caster sugar
2 banana shallots
1 sprig tarragon
200ml extra virgin olive oil

JOHN BADLEY,
EXECUTIVE HEAD CHEF,
MACDONALD LEEMING HOUSE,
WATERMILLOCK

Mix all ingredients together.

 tip.....

Makes an ideal dressing for fine beans, goat's cheese fondant or tomato jelly.

Potted Salmon
with warm potato salad

For the potted salmon:
200g fresh salmon, skinned
and cut into small dice
1 tbsp chopped shallots
100g unsalted butter
1 tbsp capers, chopped
1 tbsp chopped dill
1 tbsp chopped parsley
1 tbsp grated horseradish
half a lemon, juiced

For the potato salad:
200g small new potatoes,
washed, boiled, refreshed and
cut into quarters
2 tbsp chopped black olives
4 tbsp olive oil
4 spring onions sliced finely
1 tiny pinch of saffron

serves 4

Take just a small knob of butter and melt it in a medium sized pan, throw in the shallots and cook without colour for two minutes. Add the remaining butter and melt over a low heat.

Add the salmon and fold over gently, throw in the capers, dill, parsley, horseradish and lemon juice and allow to just warm through. The salmon will only need a minute or two.

Divide the mix into ramekins or pots and press down with the back of a spoon, and then pour over the remaining butter. Chill for at least two hours (but better overnight).

For the salad, pour the olive oil into a frying pan with the saffron, allow this to infuse for a minute or two. Then over a medium heat throw in the potatoes, olives and onions and heat through evenly.

Turn the salmon out of the pots; arrange the warm salad on a plate with the potted salmon on top and the remaining dressing drizzled around.

LUCY COOKS - THE COOKERY
SCHOOL IN THE LAKES
www.lucycooks.co.uk

Vodka Gravadlax

1 side of salmon (2lb) pin boned and skinned
1lb of rock salt
1lb of caster sugar
200ml of honey
200ml of vodka
15g fresh dill
2 whole lemons

ADRIAN WOOD, HEAD CHEF,
McMENAMINS RESTAURANT,
MARYPORT

Zest and squeeze the lemons and place into a bowl.
Mix the salt and sugar into the lemon.
Place a large strip of plastic wrap on a surface (large enough to wrap the salmon). Place $\frac{1}{2}$ of the salt, sugar and lemon mix onto the plastic wrap and place the salmon on top.
Cover the salmon with the rest of the mix, then plastic wrap and leave for 24 hours to cure in the fridge. Remove the plastic wrap, salt and sugar mix. Mix the dill (finely chopped) with the honey and vodka mix. Again place a large strip of plastic wrap on a surface (large enough to wrap the salmon into). Place the salmon into the plastic wrap and pour the honey and vodka mix over the salmon making sure you don't spill any - a tray or dish with a 1cm lip on it will help. Then cover the salmon with plastic wrap making a parcel. Turn at least 4 times over the next 15 hours.

Serving:

Unwrap the salmon and save the excess liquid for a dressing.
Slice finely on an angle as for smoked salmon.
Serve on a bed of mixed leaf lettuce with olives, sun blushed red tomatoes and parmesan shavings.
Finish with a drizzle of the liquid left over from the marinated salmon.

Sicilian Orange Bruschetta

12 cherry vine tomatoes
50g goat cheese
1 spring onion
clove garlic
olive oil
French stick
chunky orange marmalade

serves 4

Peel then crush one clove of garlic into two tablespoons of olive oil and season with salt and pepper.
Heat a large non stick pan and pre-heat a medium grill.
Meanwhile slice a French stick diagonally to get 4 large slices about 1.5cm thick.
Brush one side of the sliced bread with the garlic oil and place downwards in the hot pan and cook for a minute or so until lightly toasted.
Spread each slice with a level tablespoon of chunky, orange marmalade and cook for another minute.
Meanwhile quarter the 12 cherry vine tomatoes, slice one spring onion and dice about 50g of goat cheese.
Top the toasted bread with the tomatoes, then the diced goat cheese and finally sprinkle with spring onion.
Season to taste, drizzle a spoon of garlic oil over them and place back under the grill until the goat cheese just starts to melt.
Serve each bruschetta on a side plate garnished with a rocket salad, red onion and black olives with a drizzle of vinaigrette.

Sicily is famous for its citrus groves and blood oranges so if you can get hold of a blood orange marmalade this tasty starter or snack would be even better! The sweet marmalade works very well with the tangy vine tomatoes and salty goat cheese.

 tip.....

You can vary the amounts of the toppings to your preference, also try it with lime marmalade or sprinkled with diced crispy bacon.

RICHARD SHANNAN,
CASA ROMANA, CARLISLE.

Sicilian Orange Bruschetta (page 26)

Honey Roast Preserved Lemon Chicken (page 42)

Main Courses

Marmalade Glazed Duck with Sweet Potato Mash (page 31)

Marmalade Glazed Duck
with sweet potato mash

2 duck breasts
1 tbsp heaped marmalade
1 tbsp red wine vinegar
4 tbsp water
1 star anise
$\frac{1}{4}$ tsp 5 spice powder
(optional, adds extra oriental flavour)
serves 2

Duck is a classic. It had a bad reputation in the past as being too fatty or masked by overpowering flavours like the 1970s' 'duckling a l'orange'.
It has however maintained its appearance over the years on menus all around the globe.
Just take Chinese crispy duck with pancakes for example. We decided to use that retro idea of duck with orange and, with a nod to crispy duck give it an Asian twist. We have the dish on our menu at Zest Restaurant which has proved to be an absolute winner.
That exact recipe is quite complicated so we thought we'd give you a simpler version to tackle at home.

EMMA AND RICKY ADALCIO,
ZEST RESTAURANT,
WHITEHAVEN

Put all ingredients in a pan and heat gently until everything has blended together. This should only take a minute or two and can be done in advance.

To eliminate the fattiness from the duck the idea is to render the fat off. To do this score the fat in a criss-cross pattern with a sharp knife. Do not go too deep. Just cut the fat and not the flesh.
Heat a dry frying pan until hot but not smoking, no oil required. Season with salt and pepper and place the duck breasts fat side down and leave for approximately 5 minutes. Do not feel the need to move it around the pan, just check that it is not burning. It is allowed to go a deep golden brown but not black.
Stand back as it may spit, but be amazed by the amount of fat that seeps out. Turn the duck over and cook on the other side for a minute. Remove from pan leaving the fat behind and place on a baking tray fat side up. Spread the glaze over the duck and put in a hot oven at 200C for about another five to seven minutes depending on the size of the duck.
This should give you a lovely medium cooked meat. If you prefer it medium well to well done leave it in for a further 5 to 7 minutes. Take the meat out and leave it in a warm place to rest for five minutes. The marmalade is meant only as a flavouring glaze, it is not a sauce. If you do cook your duck medium, it will be juicy enough not to need a sauce and you can use the resting juices from the tray as they taste great.

To go with this we have a really simple mash:
Before oven cooking the duck put 1 medium size sweet potato per person in the oven and cook for 30 minutes or until soft. Cut in half and scoop out the beautiful golden flesh. Mash it up with a fork. It doesn't have to be super smooth. Add a knob of butter if you wish and season with salt and pepper. Even better is to throw in a handful of fresh chopped coriander.

 tip.....

This glaze is great with pork if you don't fancy duck. The mash is lovely with a dollop of cream cheese added to it.

Marinated Pork Fillet

2 pork fillets
2oz sprigs fresh parsley
2oz sprigs fresh oregano
$\frac{1}{2}$ tsp cumin
6 tbsp of olive oil
6 tbsp of olive oil, for cooking
1 lemon ⎫
1 lime ⎬ juice and zest
1 orange ⎭
2 minced cloves of garlic
1 medium onion (liquidised)
1 bottle Corona beer
6 tbsp of hickory BBQ sauce
salt and black pepper to taste.

serves 6

Trim any fat of the pork and cut on an angle to create 6oz portions.
Mix all ingredients together and place pork into marinade in fridge
for 4 to 6 hours.
Pan-fry pork for 5/10 minutes until cooked (make sure pork is not
over cooked. Pork must be served moist).
Turn the meat frequently so not to burn.
Serve on a *sweet potato mash with spring onions through it and
drizzle orange pesto and BBQ dressing.

*see recipe suggestion on page 31

ADRIAN WOOD, HEAD CHEF,
McMENAMINS RESTAURANT, MARYPORT

Marmalade Chicken

8 chicken thighs
4 tbsp Seville orange
marmalade
1 tbsp ginger, finely chopped
2 tsp Dijon mustard
2 garlic cloves, finely chopped
1 tsp sea salt
fresh ground black pepper
2 fl oz orange juice
1 tbsp olive oil

serves 4

MARILYN ECKTON, PRESTON

Heat the oven to 180C/350F/gas mark 4.
In a bowl, combine the marmalade, ginger, garlic, mustard, salt,
pepper, orange juice and olive oil and mix well.
Add the chicken and coat well to marinate.
Line a baking tin with kitchen foil and tip the chicken and
marinade into it, cover with foil and bake for 30 minutes.
Baste the chicken with the cooking juices/marinade in the pan
and return to the oven uncovered for 15/20 minutes more, until
nicely browned.
To garnish:
A spring onion finely chopped.
Season well and serve with salad or on a bed of mash.

Baked Golden Lemon Chicken

80g/3oz butter
1 small farmhouse loaf, crusts removed and cut into 1cm/$\frac{1}{2}$in cubes
1 medium onion, peeled and cut into rings
2 tbsp plain flour
150ml/5fl oz milk
150ml/5fl oz chicken stock
125g/4oz button mushrooms, halved
1.1kg/2$\frac{1}{2}$lb cooked chicken, cut into chunks
125g/4oz sweetcorn
juice of $\frac{1}{2}$ lemon
2 tbsp parsley, freshly chopped
salt and black pepper to taste

serves 4/6

Preheat the oven to 200C/400F/gas mark 6.
Heat 55g/2oz of the butter then stir in the bread cubes to coat. Transfer to a baking tray and cook in the oven for 10 minutes or until just beginning to brown and crisp.
Melt the remaining butter in a pan, add the onion and cook for about 15 minutes or until golden.
Stir in the flour to make a roux and cook for 1/2 minutes.
Blend in the milk and stock. Bring to the boil.
Add the mushrooms and simmer for 2 minutes.
Add the chicken, sweet corn, lemon juice, parsley, salt and pepper. Turn into an ovenproof dish.
Reduce the oven temperature to 180C/350F/gas mark 4.
Pile the bread cubes on top of chicken mixture and bake in the oven for 25/30 minutes or until the bread is a deep golden colour and the chicken is heated through.

NICK MARTIN, www.nickofthyme.co.uk

Beef, Tomato and Orange Casserole

2lb chuck or stewing steak
2 red onions, chopped
1 fat clove of garlic, crushed
2 tins of cherry tomatoes or
large punnet of fresh cherry
tomatoes plus $\frac{1}{2}$pint passata
or tomato juice
3 tbsp balsamic vinegar
2 tbsp redcurrant jelly
2 tbsp Worcester sauce
1 heaped tbsp tomato puree
1 level tsp dried basil
1 beef stock cube dissolved in
$\frac{1}{2}$ pint of boiling water
1 orange, halved

Brown the beef and place to one side.
Fry the onions and garlic for 5 minutes in butter and olive oil.
Add to beef and all other ingredients.
Season well, lots of fresh ground black pepper.
Liquid should be just below the beef level in casserole dish.
Push orange halves down into casserole.
Cover and cook slowly for $1\frac{1}{2}/2$ hours until the beef is tender and sauce reduced.
Serve with a little fresh torn basil leaves and remove orange halves before serving with olive cous cous or creamy mash and salad.

JACKIE DODDS, WREAY

Citrus Chicken Breasts

4 chicken breasts
1 orange
1 lime
1 x 3cm piece fresh root ginger
1 tbsp clear honey
2 tsp balsamic vinegar
seasoning
fresh tarragon

serves 4

tip.....

*Serve with green salad
and crusty bread.*

Put the chicken into a shallow dish.
Peel orange and lime with zest and place on top of chicken.
Grate the fresh ginger and place on top of chicken.
Squeeze orange and lime, pour juice over the chicken then add honey and vinegar.
Ensure both sides are covered then cover and refrigerate for a minimum of 1 hour.
Remove from marinade, season to taste then grill until cooked on both sides. Pour the remaining heated marinade over chicken. Garnish with freshly chopped tarragon.

SUE NICHOLSON, TRUSTEE – HOSPICE AT HOME, CARLISLE AND NORTH LAKELAND

Citrus Risotto

1 onion (finely chopped)
80g Arborio rice
30g butter
100ml white wine
juice and zest of 1 lemon
juice and zest of 1 orange
200ml hot stock (chicken or vegetable)
handful of peas (fresh or frozen)
20g fresh parmesan (grated)
dash of cream

serves 2

GEOFF AND ISABEL FERGUSON,
ACORN BANK, WETHERAL
www.acornbank.co.uk

Gently fry the onion in a little oil until soft but not coloured.
Add the rice and cook until the grains go opaque (1 min) Add the wine and cook until the rice has absorbed.
Add the lemon and orange zest followed by the juice once absorbed add the hot stock a ladle at a time until all has been absorbed.
The rice should be cooked to a creamy consistency.
Finish by adding the peas, parmesan, cream and butter.

 tip.....

Serve on its own. For a great supper dish top with confit of duck and a Madeira sauce. Serve with salmon drizzled with extra virgin olive oil or why not try for breakfast topped with a lightly poached egg and some local pancetta.

Cuban Style Marinated Lamb

4 tbsp Seville orange marmalade
3 tbsp water
2 oranges, zest only
2 tbsp oregano, finely chopped
6 cloves garlic, finely chopped
2 tsp cayenne pepper
2 tbsp vegetable oil
1.7kg/3lb 12oz butterflied leg of lamb (weight after bones removed)
225ml/8fl oz cola

serves 6

NICK MARTIN,
www.nickofthyme.co.uk

Gently heat the marmalade and water together in a pan, stirring until the marmalade has melted.
Allow to cool and then mix with the orange zest, oregano, garlic, cayenne and oil.
Rub the marinade into the lamb.
Place into a strong plastic bag and place the bag into a bowl.
Pour the cola around the meat.
Tie the top of the bag securely. NB: If you were to place the meat in a bowl there would not be sufficient cola to cover the meat, so pouring the cola in the bag means that you can massage and turn the meat easily while it is marinating in the fridge. Marinate for at least two hours.
Remove the meat from the fridge about half an hour in advance.
Remove from the plastic bag just before cooking.
Place lamb on the pre-heated barbecue and grill for about 1 hour or until tender.
Allow to rest for 15 minutes, then carve and serve.

Hake with Dill and Orange Sauce

4x 180g/6oz hake steaks
300ml/½ pint fish or chicken stock
1 tbsp fresh dill
salt and black freshly ground black pepper
2 oranges, peeled and cut into segments
1 tbsp corn flour
6 tbsp fresh orange juice
fresh dill

serves 4

Poach the hake steaks in the fish stock with the dill and seasoning for 8/10 minutes.
Drain and transfer to a warmed serving dish, reserving the poaching liquid.
Mix the cornflour to a paste with the orange juice and add to the poaching liquid.
Bring to the boil and simmer for 4/5 minutes, stirring until thickened and hot.
Spoon some of the sauce over the fish and garnish with fresh dill.

NICK MARTIN, www.nickofthyme.co.uk

La Daube de Boeuf Provençale

½oz dried porcini mushrooms
½oz butter
1 tbsp olive oil
2lb blade steak cut into slices
2cm thick
6oz bacon lardons (short, fat
strips)
1 large onion, sliced
4 garlic cloves, sliced
2 carrots, sliced on the diagonal
1 fennel bulb, trimmed and cut
into thin wedges
2 beef tomatoes, thickly sliced
pared zest of ½ small orange
15fl oz Cabernet Sauvignon
wine
bouquet garni of 2 thyme sprigs,
2 bay leaves and a small bunch
of parsley
salt and freshly ground black
pepper

For the persillade:
1 garlic clove, peeled
a good handful of parsley leaves
1 salted anchovy fillet, rinsed of
excess salt
6 capers, 2 pitted black olives

serves 6

tip.....

*Serve with mashed potatoes
and a light green salad.*

Cover the porcini mushrooms with 5fl oz hot water and leave them to soak for 20 minutes.

Preheat the oven to 140C/275F/gas mark 1.

Heat the butter and oil in a flameproof casserole. Brown the pieces of steak in batches, turning them over to achieve a uniform colour on all sides. A set of tongs is ideal for this and no kitchen should be without one. Remove the beef and set aside. Reduce the heat a little, add the bacon lardons and fry until lightly golden. Add the onion and fry until lightly browned.

Return the meat to the pan and add all the other ingredients - garlic, carrots, fennel, tomatoes, orange zest, soaked porcini mushrooms and their liquor, the red wine, bouquet garni, 1 teaspoon of salt and some pepper. Cover, transfer to the oven and cook for 3½ hours.

While the daube is cooking, make the persillade by coarsely chopping together the garlic, parsley, anchovy, capers and olives. Remove the daube from the oven, skim off all the excess fat from the surface then sprinkle with the persillade and take to the table.

"La Daube de Boeuf Provencale" From Food Heroes Another Helping by Rick Stein, Published by BBC Books. Reprinted by permission of the Random House Group Ltd

Duck Breast
with confit of leg, orange and balsamic

2 duck breasts
2 duck legs
800g duck or goose fat
50ml balsamic vinegar
150ml olive oil
1 orange, zest and juice
salt and pepper to season

serves 2

For the confit:

Place the 2 duck legs in a roasting tin, with duck or goose fat, add salt, a bay leaf, pink peppercorns, 2 sprigs of fresh thyme.
Place in a preheated oven at 140C gas mark 2 for 4 hours.
Remove from the heat, put to one side, and leave to cool.
Remove all meat from bone, discard bones and skin. Finely shred the meat.
In a medium saucepan heat the olive oil, balsamic vinegar, zest and juice of the orange. When the mixture is hot, add the meat and stir in. Leave to simmer for 10 minutes.
Remove from the heat.
Remove the meat from the sauce and place the meat into 2 greased and lined ramekin moulds or something similar.
Reserve the sauce for later.
Cover with cling film. This can be done the day before.

Duck breasts:

Cook the duck breasts in a frying pan, skin side down firstly for 5 minutes on a medium heat until the skin is golden and crispy. Season then turn and cook for a further 4 minutes. Take the duck breasts out of pan and rest for up to 15 minutes.

To serve:

Gently reheat confit of leg in oven at 140C or gas mark 2 for 8 minutes place in middle of the dinner/serving plate. Slice duck breast in 2/3 pieces and place on top of the confit, dress with the olive oil and balsamic orange used for the confit leg.

tip.....

Serve with boiled potatoes and roast butternut squash.

GAVIN IRVING, HEAD CHEF,
CROSBY LODGE HOTEL

Grilled Squid
with lime and noodles

1 tbsp olive oil
200g/7oz squid, cleaned and cut into rings
salt and freshly ground black pepper
2 garlic cloves, finely chopped
$\frac{1}{2}$ red chilli, finely chopped
$\frac{1}{2}$ stalk lemongrass, finely chopped
2 limes, juice only
1 tbsp soy sauce
2 tsp sesame oil
100g/$3\frac{1}{2}$oz egg noodles, cooked and drained
1 free range egg, beaten
1 tsp caster sugar
2 tbsp chopped fresh coriander (reserve some for garnish)

serves 4

Rub the squid in olive oil and season with salt and freshly ground black pepper.

Heat a griddle pan until smoking hot. Add the squid and cook for 1/2 minutes, shaking the pan continuously until chargrilled on all sides. Remove from the heat and keep warm.

Heat a little olive oil in a sauté pan, add the chilli, garlic and lemongrass and cook gently for one minute.

Add the lime juice, soy, sesame oil and egg noodles. Stir well and then add the beaten egg and sugar. Cook for 1/2 minutes, stirring to coat the noodles in the egg. Stir in most of the coriander.

To serve, place a pile of noodles on a plate and top with the squid. Garnish with the remaining coriander.

NICK MARTIN, www.nickofthyme.co.uk

Herb Crusted Pork Loin Steaks

4 large (or 8 small) pork loin steaks
olive oil
3 slices white bread (crusts removed)
grated zest of 1 lime
juice of 1 lime
1 tsp dried tarragon
1 tsp dried rosemary
orange marmalade
lime marmalade
1 red onion
2/3 tbsp balsamic vinegar
½ glass good red wine
12 cherry vine tomatoes

serves 4

Seal the seasoned pork loin steaks in a hot pan with olive oil until they take on a nice colour, then remove from the heat and leave to cool slightly.

While the pork is resting, preheat oven to 180C.

Blend 3 slices of white bread (crusts removed) with the grated zest of 1 lime, a spoon of dried tarragon and a spoon of dried rosemary and a pinch of salt.

Spread the pork steaks with orange marmalade and then press the bread mix firmly on top. Place in the hot oven and bake for 10 minutes until crispy.

Fry a finely sliced red onion in a non stick pan until golden brown. Add a large tablespoon of lime marmalade, the juice of the lime, 2/3 tbsps of balsamic vinegar and half a glass of good red wine. Bring to the boil and reduce by half, then throw in 12 cherry vine tomatoes and simmer to a sticky syrup (if it reduces too much just add a bit of water or stock).

Serve the steaks on warm plates and drizzle with sauce.

TIM BAUGH, CASA ROMANA RESTAURANT, CARLISLE

tip.....

Try substituting different meats, lamb or duck work particularly well, or different herbs that you may prefer.

Serve with creamy pesto mashed potatoes and sautéed garlic spinach, or on a bed of tossed, buttered spaghetti.

Herdwick Lamb
with seasonal vegetables and a Cumberland sauce

Herdwick lamb:
1 boned leg of Herdwick lamb
(approx 1lb)

Cumberland sauce:
zest and juice of one lemon
zest and juice of one orange
400g redcurrant jelly
325ml port
2 cloves garlic (roughly chopped)
1 tbsp grated fresh ginger
200g raisins
1 shallot (finely chopped)

Seasonal vegetables:
broccoli
baby new potatoes
French beans

CHRIS MEREDITH, GILPIN
LODGE, WINDERMERE

Seal the lamb and place in a very hot oven (250C) for 35 minutes. Take out and let it rest for 10 minutes.

To make the Cumberland sauce mix the lemon juice and zest with redcurrant jelly, port and bring to the boil. Add the rest of the ingredients and bring to coating consistency.
Can be served warm or chilled.

Cook baby new potatoes, broccoli and French beans in salted water as normal. Serve potatoes with unsalted butter and fresh mint. Toss the cooked beans in butter, salt and pepper and add some roasted finely chopped shallots.

tip.....

Pour a generous helping of Cumberland sauce over carved lamb and dress with seasonal vegetables.

Lemoncello Gin Swizzle

2 measures Plymouth gin
2 measures lemoncello
1 measure of fresh lemon juice
2 dashes Angostura bitters
1 scoop of crushed ice

Blend together, gin, lemoncello, fresh lemon juice and Angostura bitters, then pour into a tall glass filled with crushed ice.
Serve with a swizzle stick.

PIPPA SEDGWICK, PHILIPPA SEDGWICK WINES

Honey Roast Preserved Lemon Chicken

For the marinade:

2/3 preserved organic lemons
juice of half a lemon
2 cloves of garlic, chopped
handful of parsley
1 tsp of cumin seeds
1 tsp of sweet paprika
4 tbsp olive oil
handful of sage
honey to taste

Ingredients to cook:

1kg chicken, thighs and legs
1 medium white onion
olive oil
50g butter
100ml Vermouth

serves 4

MARTIN CAMPBELL,
www.artisan-food.com

Wash the preserved lemons, (see page 17), remove and discard all pith, then rough chop the peel. Place all the marinade ingredients into the blender and blitz until sticky paste. Add olive oil as necessary to achieve this consistency. Add sufficient honey to get a balance between the citrus flavour and the sweetness. Once you are happy with the sweetness level rub the marinade into the chicken pieces and put in a fridge overnight.

Pour a little olive oil and butter into a large pot. When the butter has melted and the oil is hot, add the chopped onions, sweat them until starting to turn very slightly golden. Remove the chicken pieces from the marinade, cleaning off most of it and seal them in the butter/onion mix. Once sealed, add the vermouth, let it bubble for a while until reduced slightly, then add the marinade from the chicken pieces. Ensure there is enough fluid to cover the chicken, if not add some water. Put the pot on a very low heat with the lid removed. Once the chicken is cooked, maybe after 20/30 minutes of simmering, remove the chicken pieces and keep them warm. Reduce the remaining liquid until it is a medium/thick consistency. Taste and check seasoning as well as sweetness. Once happy and ready to serve, add the chicken plus juices back to the pot and serve once fully re-heated. Serve with boiled potatoes garnished with chopped parsley butter and seasoning.

Hot Spiced Chicken
with lemon juice

3lb (1.4kg) roasting chicken
1 tbsp (15ml) salt
3 cloves of garlic, crushed
$\frac{1}{2}$ teaspoon cayenne pepper
1 teaspoon turmeric
3 tbsps (45ml) olive oil or
melted butter
2 medium onions, finely
chopped
4 cloves
2 teaspoons cumin seeds
1 teaspoon coriander seeds
2 tbsps (30ml) tomato puree
6fl oz (175ml) water
juice of 2 lemons

Preparation time
1 hour 45 minutes
serves 4-6

Cut the chicken into serving pieces and wipe them dry. Combine the salt, garlic, cayenne pepper and turmeric, and rub the mixture into the skin side of the chicken pieces. Leave for 15 minutes.

Heat the oil or melted butter in a large, heavy frying pan and brown the chicken on both sides. Remove the pieces to a plate and in the same oil lightly fry the chopped onions until just soft. Stir in the cloves, cumin and coriander seeds and continue frying. After a few minutes stir in the tomato puree and return the chicken pieces to the pan. Add the water, cover the pan tightly, and simmer very gently for 1 hour or until the chicken is tender. Rest for 45 minutes, add the lemon juice and adjust the seasoning to taste.

JUDY GOPSILL, COMPLEMENTARY THERAPIST, HOSPICE AT HOME, CARLISLE AND NORTH LAKELAND

Pink Grapefruitade

6 pink grapefruits
2 lemons
2lb sugar lumps

Rub the zest of the grapefruit and lemons with sugar lumps. Put the sugar into a jug and pour 4 pints of boiling water over it. Add the juice of the grapefruits and lemons, stir well, and allow to cool. Strain and serve.

PIPPA SEDGWICK, PHILIPPA SEDGWICK WINES

Lemon and Sweet Potato Roast Chicken

2 juicy lemons, halved lengthways & thinly sliced
1 large free range or corn-fed chicken (cut into pieces)
150ml good quality olive oil
1kg (2.5lb approx) sweet potatoes (parsnips make a good alternative) peeled and cut into 2cm or 1 inch dice
1 garlic bulb, unpeeled, halved into 2 rounds
1 red onion, peeled and cut into wedges
2 tsp fresh rosemary leaves
2 tsp fresh oregano leaves
salt and freshly ground pepper

serves 4

MATT LUCAS, HEAD CHEF,
THE GATE INN, YANWATH

Preheat oven to 220C/gas mark 7. Remove chicken legs and cut each into two through the joint, separating thigh from drumstick. Remove the wings and supremes and cut these into two as well. Keep the carcase for stock to be used for another occasion.
Mix the diced sweet potatoes and red onions with the herbs, a little salt and pepper and half the oil, place in roasting dish. Brown the chicken pieces with a little olive oil in a frying pan and the two halves of the garlic bulb.
Put the leg joints on top of the sweet potatoes and scatter the lemon pieces over them. Roast for 25/30 minutes.
Add the supreme pieces (as these don't want to become dry), drizzle with the remaining oil and roast for a further 20/30 mins. The chicken is ready when the juices run clear when the flesh is pricked.

This is a dish packed with flavour and reminds me of my time out in Australia and New Zealand and is a variation on the dish we used to cook for lunch in a Dunedin restaurant with the sweet, juicy lemons running through the whole dish as it roasts. It's easy to prepare and great any time of the year but I love it in the summer and is best eaten with a crunchy salad with plump olives. Use good quality, locally sourced chicken.

Waitby School Buttery Lemon Poached Chicken

with roasted vegetables

1 whole lemon

1 lemon (cut in half and one teaspoon of lemon zest)

1 pack of fresh tarragon (20g)

2 bay leaves

10 shallots

4 cloves garlic

1 butternut squash

1 large leek

2 sticks celery

3 large carrots

3 tsp English mustard

400ml chicken stock

30g butter

1 tbsp olive oil

1 tbsp flour

$\frac{3}{4}$ bottle very dry white wine.

serves 6

tip.....

This is great served with jacket potatoes, finely shredded, buttered and peppered Savoy cabbage and lots of wine.

EMILY BROOM, WAITBY
SCHOOL, KIRKBY STEPHEN

Preheat the oven to 180C.

Put a tbsp of olive oil and a generous knob of butter in a heavy roasting pot (with lid) on a high heat. Chop the carrots, squash, leek and celery into cubes (about two inches square). Peel the shallots (keep them whole) and peel the garlic cloves, reserving two cloves for the chicken. Brown the vegetables, shallots and two cloves of garlic in the roasting tin. When browned, add the mustard powder and stir until everything is coated. Season with salt and pepper and add the white wine and chicken stock. Bring to the boil and simmer, then add the lemon zest. Take the chicken and insert knobs of butter and some of the tarragon leaves under the skin. Season with salt and pepper. Insert the lemon halves and two garlic cloves into the chicken's body cavity, along with more tarragon. Place the chicken in the pot and arrange the vegetables around the outside of it. The chicken should be nearly covered by the liquid. Put in the remaining tarragon, tied in a bunch. Season. Cook gently, with the lid on, in the oven for one and a half hours until the chicken juices run clear. Remove chicken, take out one half of the lemon from the body cavity, cover the chicken and allow to rest. Turn oven up to 230C. Strain vegetables and place in a roasting tin, then drizzle with olive oil and place in oven to roast for approximately half an hour, turning regularly.

Meanwhile, strain the sauce through a sieve, add two bay leaves and bring to the boil in a pan on the hob. Some of the lemon juice from the cooked lemon can be squeezed into the sauce at this stage. Mix a large knob of butter and the tbsp of flour into a beurre maniere. Once the sauce has been reduced by a third, lower the heat to a simmer and add beurre maniere gradually, while whisking. Simmer sauce to thicken and season to taste. Remove bay leaves before serving.

A flexible dish that can be cooked either quickly and then left alone in the oven, or can be taken at a slower pace, requiring the consumption of quite a few bottles of wine and the presence of a lot of friends in the kitchen. The chicken is succulent and gently fragranced with lemon and tarragon, contrasting beautifully with the golden vegetables. The vegetables can, of course, be varied according to the season. Fresh thyme can be used as a substitute for tarragon.

Orange Braised Lamb Shanks

4 lamb shanks
2 carrots, diced finely
2 medium onions, diced finely
2 celery sticks, diced finely
30/45ml or 2/3 tbsp olive oil
few sprigs fresh thyme
2 bay leaves
4 garlic cloves, finely chopped
3 oranges, juice and finely grated zest (no pith)
1 lemon, juice and finely grated zest (no pith)
4 tbsp tomato puree
$\frac{1}{2}$ bottle white wine
250ml/8$\frac{1}{2}$fl oz lamb stock (or water)
salt and pepper
fresh parsley, chopped

serves 4

In a suitable casserole dish, sweat the diced vegetables in some of the olive oil, without browning, until tender.

Add the thyme, bay leaves, garlic, tomato, wine and lamb stock or water, along with most of the orange zest and juice (retain a few pinches of zest and 1 tbsp of juice). Bring to the boil and lower to a gentle simmer.

Heat a little more olive oil in a separate pan and brown the lamb shanks on all sides, seasoning with a little salt and pepper as you go.

Transfer to the casserole dish and cover with its lid. Cook in a preheated slow-moderate oven (about 150C/300F/gas mark 2) until the meat is completely tender and coming off the bone.

Remove the shanks from the pan and keep warm while you finish the sauce. Skim off some of the fat that is floating on it. Taste for seasoning and to assess its intensity. Boil to reduce if you think it needs it.

Stir in the reserved juice to refresh the citrus flavour.

Serve one lamb shank on each warmed plate with a generous amount of sauce spooned over. Sprinkle each shank with a little parsley and a pinch of the reserved zest.

NICK MARTIN, www.nickofthyme.co.uk

Pork in a Mustard Sauce

300g pork fillet, sliced thinly
25g butter
45ml water
125ml single cream
salt and pepper
juice of one orange
1 tbsp Dijon mustard (not English as it is too strong)

serves 4

Rub seasoning into pork fillet and fry slowly in the butter until it is browned on both sides and cooked right through.

Remove and keep warm, covered, in a low oven.

Add the orange juice and water to the pan juices and bring to the boil. Remove from the heat. Add the mustard and stir in well. Finish off with the cream.

Pour over the pork and serve with potatoes and vegetables.

JUDITH WILSON, LANGWATHBY

Orange Braised Lamb Shanks (page 46)

Shrimp and Herb Risotto

50g/2oz butter
1 large onion, finely chopped
1 clove garlic
120ml/4fl oz dry white wine
900ml/2 pints hot stock (vegetable or fish)
250g/9oz Arborio rice
more butter
lots of fresh parsley and chives
1 lemon
500g/1lb Solway brown shrimps

serves 4

Melt the 50g butter in a pan and add the onion and fry for 5/10 minutes until the onion is soft and lightly browned. Add the garlic and continue to cook slowly for another 5 minutes. Add the rice and turn it over until all the grains are coated in the oniony butter. Pour in the wine and bring to a simmer, stir well. Heat the stock in another saucepan nearby and ladle a little at a time into the rice pan, stirring well until it has all been absorbed before adding more.
Continue cooking gently like this until the stock has been used and the rice is tender and creamy but still has a bite.
Stir in the shrimps and a little more butter with the herbs and a squeeze of lemon to taste. Dish in individual bowls with more herbs and shrimps to garnish.

ANNETTE GIBBONS, COOKERY PRESENTER AND PATRON — HOSPICE AT HOME, CARLISLE AND NORTH LAKELAND
www.cumbriaonaplate.co.uk

Venison in a Sticky Citrus Sauce

1 tbsp of marmalade, without rind if possible and not too bitter
venison fastfry or stirfry
juice of 1 orange
juice of 1 lemon
1 tbsp of tomato ketchup
glass of sherry
a pinch of cinnamon
pinch of nutmeg
2 cloves

JANE EMMERSON
DEER 'N DEXTER, PENRUDDOCK

If using fastfry cut into thin strips. Combine all the above and place the meat strips in it. Leave the meat to marinade for an hour or so. Heat some oil and butter in a wide pan on a high heat. Lift the meat from the marinade and flash fry in the hot oil over a high heat. Remove the meat after 30/45 seconds, place on a warmed plate and cover with tin foil or place the plate in a warm oven. Add more meat and continue until all the meat is cooked. Leave the meat resting in the warm, where it will continue to cook, add the marinade to the pan, simmer and reduce until the sauce is a good coating consistency. Return the meat to the pan, toss in the sauce, re-heat the meat for a few seconds if necessary.

Serve over rice or cous cous.

Venison in a Sticky Citrus Sauce (page 48)

No.15 Spicy Fishcakes
on bed of noodles with crème fraiche and lime

Spicy sauce:
1 inch of fresh ginger
1 red chilli
8 tbsp soy sauce
$\frac{1}{4}$ pint of water
1 tbsp sugar
juice of 1 lime
3 cloves garlic
1 stick lemongrass

Fishcakes:
500g cooked flaked fish, eg
salmon and cod
500g mashed potato
1 small bunch chives, finely
chopped
1 red chilli, finely diced
seasoning

For the noodles:
1 red pepper, finely sliced
1 yellow pepper, finely sliced
4 spring onions, finely sliced
$\frac{1}{2}$ red onion, finely sliced
2 red chillies, finely diced

Garnish:
1 tbsp crème fraiche, 1 lime
wedge, fresh coriander.

No. 15 CAFÉ BAR AND
GALLERY, PENRITH

Spicy sauce:
Place all of the ingredients in a pan and simmer gently for 15
minutes then strain sauce into a jug.

Fishcakes:
Combine all ingredients, adding 2 tbsps of the sauce.
Shape into fishcakes, lightly dust in flour and place in fridge.

Noodles:
Cook the noodles until just softened. Drain.
Pan fry the fishcakes on a low heat for 3 minutes each side.
Using one tbsp of oil, sauté the vegetables. When coloured add the
noodles to the pan with the remainder of the sauce and cook on a
high heat for 2/3 minutes and stir fry.

Garnish:
Create a bed of the noodles and vegetables in the centre of the
plate. Place the fishcakes on top of the noodles. Garnish with
1 tbsp of crème fraiche, a wedge of fresh lime and fresh coriander.

Seville Orange and Soy Sauce Marinated Pheasant Breasts

6 pheasant breasts
2 tbsp olive oil
2oz butter
6 banana shallots or 12 smaller ones, skinned and finely chopped.
2 cloves garlic, skinned and finely chopped
1 tsp arrowroot, slaked with 2 tbsp cold water
sea salt
pepper

For the marinade:

1 pint fresh orange juice, to include the juice of 1 Seville orange
a good grating of nutmeg
$\frac{1}{2}$ tsp cinnamon
2 tbsp honey
$\frac{1}{2}$ pint red wine
3 tbsp best soy sauce
zest of 1 Seville orange.

serves 6

Arrange the pheasant breasts in a dish large enough to hold them and the marinade.

Make the marinade by heating half of the orange juice with the spices and honey. When the honey has melted into the juice take the pan off the heat and pour in the rest of the orange juice, with the red wine and soy sauce.

Stir in the orange zest, and pour the marinade over the pheasant breasts. Leave them to marinate for at least 24 hours.

When you are ready to cook them, lift the breasts out of the marinade and pat them dry with absorbent kitchen paper.

Heat the oil and the butter together in a sauté pan, and cook the breasts over a moderate heat for about 5 minutes or until they are cooked through. Then lay them in a warm serving dish.

Add the shallots and the garlic to the sauté pan and cook, stirring, for 4/5 minutes, until the shallots are very soft. Pour in the marinade and let it bubble furiously, to reduce by about a third. Stir some of the hot sauce into the slaked arrowroot, pour this back into the saucepan, and stir until the sauce bubbles.

Taste, and season with salt and pepper. Pour the sauce over the pheasant breasts in the warm serving dish, cover with a lid or some foil and keep the dish warm until you are ready to serve. It will keep warm without spoiling for up to 30 minutes.

LADY CLAIRE MACDONALD, AWARD-WINNING COOK AND FOOD WRITER, KINLOCH LODGE, ISLE OF SKYE
www.claire-macdonald.com

Lemongrass Granitae (page 57)

Puddings

Baked Apple Soufflé (page 55)

Baked Apple Soufflé
with white chocolate & Kirsch Sauce

Marmalade sauce:
120g lime marmalade
15ml cornflour
splash of Kirsch

Large baking apples:
6 large unpeeled
Granny Smith or Braeburn
apples
100g butter
100g grated dark chocolate
icing sugar

Soufflé Mixture:
8 egg whites whisked until stiff

White Chocolate sauce:
300g white chocolate
400ml double cream
35ml Kirsch

serves 6

Slowly heat marmalade and add splash of Kirsch. Mix the cornflour in a little cold water until dissolved. Add to the marmalade mix and allow to cool.

Slice across the top quarter of each apple. Hollow out contents leaving 1cm of apple attached to the skin. Grease the insides with soft butter. Sprinkle with freshly grated dark chocolate.

Whisk the egg whites until stiff and peaking then gently fold into the marmalade mixture. Spoon inside individual apples and place in fridge until set.

Score around the inside of the apple to release the mixture from the edges.

Bake in oven for 8/10 minutes at 180C. Dust with icing sugar.

Melt the white chocolate slowly and add Kirsch and cream together.

Serve sauce with apples

JEAN CHRISTOPHE NOVELLI - THE NATION'S FAVOURITE FRENCH CHEF

 tip.....

When emptying apple with spoon turn them over for 10 mins to release out the juice.

Citrus Tart

Pate sucrée:

9oz (275g) plain flour
$5\frac{1}{2}$oz (165g) butter
$3\frac{1}{2}$oz (100g) icing sugar
small pinch of salt
1 egg and 1 yolk
1/2 drops of vanilla extract

Filling:

4 large eggs
$10\frac{1}{2}$oz (315g) caster sugar
zest of $\frac{1}{2}$ large orange
4floz (125ml) fresh lemon juice
4floz (125ml) fresh orange juice
4floz (125ml) double cream

To serve:

$1\frac{1}{2}$/2 tbsp icing sugar, 1 lemon, rind and pith removed, flesh cut into segments between membranes

serves 8-10

For the pate sucrée, sift the flour onto a work surface and make a well in the centre. Cut butter into small pieces, place them in the centre and work them with your fingertips until completely softened. Add the sugar and salt, mix well together using fingertips, then mix in the eggs and vanilla. Gradually draw the flour into the mixture and then knead with the heel of your hand until completely homogeneous. Draw together and form into a ball, flatten the top slightly, wrap in cling film and refrigerate until very firm (for at least 2 hours). Roll out pate sucrée, line a lightly buttered 11 inch flan tin with a fluted edge and with a removable base (reserving a small amount of pate sucrée) and trim edge. Chill again wrapped in cling film for at least 1 hour until firm. Prick pate sucrée lightly with a fork, line with greaseproof paper or foil and fill with dried beans, ensuring placed right up to the edge. Bake blind for about 10 minutes in the middle of a preheated oven at 220C/gas mark 6. Remove the dried beans and greaseproof paper or foil. Fill in holes from pricking using the reserved uncooked pate sucrée (if necessary) and bake for a further 10 minutes or until lightly coloured.

Meanwhile for the filling process eggs, sugar and zest in a food processor (using a metal blade) for about a minute, until mixture is light yellow and fluffy. Add the fruit juices and cream with the machine still running, taking care not to over mix. Pour the filling into the cooled pastry crust and bake for about 5/10 minutes at 190C/ gas mark 5 or until the custard begins to set. Reduce oven temperature to 180C/gas mark 4 and bake for about 12/14 minutes longer. Remove tart from oven when filling is browned and moves only slightly when the tin is shaken. Preheat grill adjusting rack about 4 inches below the heat. Sprinkle icing sugar through a sieve uniformly over tart's surface. Arrange lemon segments on top in a circular pattern. Place tart under grill, checking every few seconds, and turning tart so that it browns evenly. When the entire surface is brown after about $1/1\frac{1}{2}$ minutes remove tart. Let it cool to room temperature before turning out and serving. The pastry and filling can be prepared separately ahead of time but the tart can only be finished a few hours before serving.

This is a complicated recipe but well worth the effort.

YVONNE MARPLES, ORTON

Lemongrass Granitae

2 litre water
500g sugar
180g glucose
juice of 4 lemons
16 lemongrass
zest of 2 lemons

serves 8

Boil sugar, water and glucose.
Add remaining ingredients
leave to infuse. Chill and fork.

JOHN BADLEY,
EXECUTIVE HEAD CHEF,
MACDONALD LEEMING HOUSE

Very Best Lemon Ice Cream

3 juicy lemons, preferably
unwaxed
175g/6oz icing sugar
425ml/¾ pint double cream,
chilled

Using a fine grater, grate the zest from two of the lemons and
squeeze the juice from all three.
Combine the zest, juice and sugar.
Whip the cream with 3 tablespoons of iced water until it holds soft
peaks, then whisk in the sweetened lemon juice.
Turn the mixture into a shallow freezer tray or freezer proof indi-
vidual serving dishes.
Cover and still freeze, without stirring, until firm.

JOAN NICHOLLS, DALSTON

Baked Lemon Pudding

50g butter
125g soft brown sugar
zest and juice of one lemon
two eggs, separated
225ml milk
50g wholemeal flour

serves 4

Set oven to 150C. Grease a pudding dish. Cream together butter, sugar and lemon zest. Beat egg yolks in slowly. When mixed, beat in lemon juice and milk. Fold in flour with metal spoon. Whisk egg white until stiff and fold into mixture. Bake in a water bath in oven until firm (about 45 minutes).

LANCRIGG COUNTRY HOUSE,
GRASMERE

Baked Orange Soufflés

4 large oranges
1 lemon
30g/1oz unsalted butter
30g/1oz plain flour
45g/1½oz caster sugar
3 free range eggs

serves 4

tip.....

*Buy organic oranges for best
flavour and no chemicals.
If the oranges are really sweet
you can omit the sugar
completely from the recipe.
The finished soufflés will "hold"
well in a slow oven for
30 minutes before serving.*

ANNETTE GIBBONS, COOKERY
PRESENTER AND PATRON -
HOSPICE AT HOME, CARLISLE
AND NORTH LAKELAND
www.cumbriaonaplate.co.uk

Scrub the oranges and cut them in half crossways. Remove the flesh and pith and cut a small slice from the base so that each half will stand up. Set the shells aside.

Extract the juice and strain it into a bowl with the lemon juice. Melt the butter in a heavy based pan and stir in the flour. Cook for a few minutes then gradually add the fruit juice, stirring continuously. This sauce should thicken as it comes to the boil. Simmer for 2 minutes then remove the pan from the heat. Stir in the sugar and let it cool.

Separate the eggs and beat one yolk at a time into the sauce, stirring well before adding the next. Whisk the egg whites until stiff and fold them into the sauce using a metal spoon. Fill the orange shells with the mixture. Place them in an ovenproof dish and bake in a preheated oven 200ºC/400ºF, gas mark 6 for about 20 minutes.   Serve the oranges dusted with sifted icing sugar.

Marmalade and Chocolate Whisky Tartlets

For the pastry

6oz flour

3oz caster sugar

half teaspoon of salt

3oz butter chopped into small pieces

2 large egg yolks

For the tartlet filling

juice of half an orange

2oz sugar

4oz grated bitter chocolate

3floz of double cream,

1 tbsp of butter

2 tbsp whisky

3 tbsp Seville orange marmalade

1 tbsp roughly chopped flaked almonds (optional)

tip.....

Sprinkle them with a few chopped flaked almonds as a garnish. The tartlets are best eaten fresh on the same day they are made.

IVAN DAY - FOOD HISTORIAN
www.historicfood.com

To make the pastry:

Sift the flour onto a board or slab. Make a well in the centre. Put the butter, salt, sugar and egg yolks into this well. Using the tips of the fingers of one hand, blend butter, salt sugar and eggs together into a sticky mass. Using a palette knife, gradually push flour into the well a little at a time, blending it in with your fingers. It will be a little difficult to handle at first and become rather dry looking. But persevere and the ingredients will start to come together. Stop the flour from spreading over your work surface with your palette knife. Once the ingredients have more or less formed into a rough pastry, start blending it by pushing it with the ball of your hand along the slab a little bit at a time. Pick up loose bits of flour with the pastry. Once all the ingredients are thoroughly blended, the pastry should resemble yellow marzipan. Put in a plastic bag and leave in a cool place (not a refrigerator) to rest for half an hour. Heat the oven to 180C. Butter eight $3^1/_2$ inch (8 cm tartlet moulds). After it has rested, divide the pastry up into eight equal-sized balls. Flatten them and roll out with a rolling pin into rounds a little larger than four inches. Cut them into perfect circles with a 4 inch scalloped pastry cutter. Line the tartlet moulds with these rounds. Prick them over lightly with a fork and put them to chill in the fridge for about 10 minutes. Crumple up eight 5 inch square pieces of baking paper. Flatten out the paper again and line your pastry cases with it. Fill each of them with some rice, lentils or split peas. Put them all on a baking tray and bake for about 7 minutes, or until the pastry rims start to brown. Remove the paper, rice etc. and put back into the oven again until they are golden brown, which will take about another 6/7 mins. Don't remove the tartlet cases from the moulds until they are completely cool.

To make the tartlet filling:

Thoroughly blend the marmalade with one tablespoonful of whisky. Spread equal amounts of this mixture over the base of each tartlet case. Put the grated chocolate into a small bowl. Put the strained orange juice and sugar into a saucepan. Put this over a low heat and stir until dissolved. Let it boil for a couple of minutes, then stir in the butter and cream until the butter melts. Bring the mixture just up to boiling point and immediately take off the heat. Pour this over the chocolate. Leave it for 1 minute to allow the chocolate to melt and stir until it becomes very smooth. Stir in the remaining tablespoon of whisky. Pour this over the marmalade in your tart cases. Tap the cases gently on the table to allow the chocolate to get an even surface and allow them to cool for half an hour.

William Caird's Cream D'Arcy

1 pint of whipping cream
4oz of Seville orange marmalade
3oz of caster sugar
the juice of a Seville orange (if not available lemon juice will do)
1 tbsp of Maraschino or Kirsch liqueur

Blend half a pint of the cream, marmalade, juice, liqueur and sugar together in an electric blender. Put into an ice cream machine and churn.

Whip the rest of the cream until it stands in peaks. When the ice cream is a semi-frozen batter add the whipped cream to it and continue to churn until fully frozen.

IVAN DAY - FOOD HISTORIAN
www.historicfood.com

Orange Jelly Baskets

1 orange per person
orange jelly
freshly squeezed orange juice
tinned mandarin orange segments, drained
some pretty ribbon

Cut a slice from the bottom of each orange so they sit comfortably. Then cut two quarter segments out of each orange half way down so you end up with a handle for your basket.
Scoop out all the orange (squeeze out juice to add to jelly) so you end up with your basket.
Make up jelly using half water and half juice.
Place some mandarin segments in each orange basket and top with jelly.
Put in the refrigerate to set. Decorate with a ribbon bow and piped cream if you want to go over the top.

YVONNE MARPLES, ORTON

Banniet Tort

For the pancake mixture:

4oz sifted plain flour
a pinch of grated nutmeg
a pinch of salt
2 eggs
7floz milk mixed with
3floz water
2oz butter

For the tort:

two sheets of rolled puff
pastry to line a deep 8 inch
tart tin and another round to
make an 8 inch cover
4oz caster sugar
1oz of finely chopped
preserved orange peel
1oz of finely chopped
preserved lemon peel
1oz of finely chopped
preserved citron peel
2 tablespoons of orange
flower water
3 tablespoons of sherry or
marsala
juice of 1 Seville orange
(if unavailable use the juice
of a lemon)
an egg yolk whisked with
a pinch of salt to glaze the
pastry

Sift the flour, salt and nutmeg into a large bowl and make a well in the centre. Put the eggs into this and whisk them with a small balloon whisk. Gradually add a little of the milk/water mixture at a time. The lumps will vanish when all the mixture is well whisked and amalgamated. When it is a smooth batter, melt the butter in a pan and thoroughly stir two tablespoons of it into the batter as this stops the pancakes sticking. Spread a little of the butter onto the base of a 7 inch frying pan and fry the pancakes as usual. About 2 tablespoons of batter poured into the buttered frying pan from a ladle is about the right amount. When they are cooked on one side, turn them and cook them for a short time on another. When they are all done, put them aside to cool.

Butter an eight-inch deep tart tin and line with a thin round of puff pastry. Put in the fridge to cool for half an hour.

Preheat the oven to 180C. Mix the orange flower water, sherry and juice together. Put one of the pancakes in the bottom of the pastry case. Sprinkle on it a little of the mixed peel, a teaspoon or two of the orange flower water mixture and a scattering of sugar. Put another pancake on top of this and repeat until the tort is full of alternate layers of pancakes and peel. Wet the edge of the pastry case and cover with another round of puff pastry. Brush the top of the tort with the egg/salt mixture and bake for 35/40 minutes. Serve with cream.

Adapted from *The Complete Practical Cook* by Charles Carter, published in 1730. It looks spectacular when cut through. Its multi-layers are full of Georgian Age flavours.

IVAN DAY - FOOD HISTORIAN
www.historicfood.com

Key Lime Pie

For the base:
95g butter
225g digestive biscuits
(crushed)

For the filling:
3 egg yolks
400g condensed milk
150ml fresh lime juice
1 level tbsp grated lime zest

serves 6

Melt butter, mix with biscuits then press into a flan tin.
Place eggs and lime zest in a bowl, mix with hand mixer for 3/4 minutes then add milk and whisk again for 3/4 minutes.
Finally add the lime juice and pour into a 6 inch flan tin.
Bake for 20 minutes at 180C.
Cool completely and serve with cream, ice cream or crème fraiche.

ALISON CRESSWELL,
AMBLESIDE

Doreen's Christmas Pudding

4oz currants

4oz sultanas

8oz raisins

2oz mixed peel

2oz cherries, chopped

2oz blanched almonds, chopped

4oz fresh breadcrumbs (white or brown)

1 medium carrot, peeled and grated

1 small cooking apple, peeled and grated

4oz shredded suet

2oz dried apricots, chopped

1oz glace ginger, chopped

4oz Demerara sugar

$\frac{1}{2}$ tsp mixed spice

$\frac{3}{4}$ tsp ground cinnamon

$\frac{1}{4}$ tsp grated nutmeg

juice and grated rind of 1 lemon

grated rind of 1 orange

4oz syrup

2 eggs

4 tbsp brown ale

2 tbsp brandy

Put all dry ingredients into a bowl and mix in carrot, apple, lemon and orange rinds.

Mix together lemon juice, syrup, eggs, brandy and brown ale and add to the mixture and stir well until evenly blended. The mixture should be soft, if it's too dry add more ale.

Grease well 1 x 2pt basin and 1 x 1pt basin. Cover with grease-proof paper then foil and tie securely with string making a handle to lift the puddings easily out of the pan.

I use a pressure cooker and steam them for 40 minutes then cook at 15lb pressure for about $2^{1}2/3$ hours. Or steam for six to eight hours. Reduce pressure slowly. When cold remove coverings and replace with fresh ones. Store in a cool, dry place until needed.

DOREEN HEAD, BECKERMET WI

Glazed Oranges with Vanilla Yoghurt

2 tbsp butter
4 tbsp brown sugar
2 oranges, peeled and sliced
1 pear, peeled and sliced
pinch of cinnamon
25ml/1floz brandy
100g/3½oz Greek yoghurt
1 vanilla pod, seeds scraped out

serves 2

NICK MARTIN,
www.nickofthyme.co.uk

Melt the butter with the brown sugar in a saucepan and cook for one minute until golden.
Add the sliced oranges and pears and the ground cinnamon and stir well to coat.
Add the brandy and carefully allow to flame. Cook for two minutes.
In a bowl, mix the Greek yoghurt and the vanilla seeds together.
To serve, place the caramelised oranges and pears on a serving plate and spoon over the vanilla yoghurt.

Lemon Posset

1 pint whipping cream
2 lemons
6oz granulated sugar

serves about 6

JANE BINNS, HEAD CHEF
ROTHAY MANOR, AMBLESIDE

Grate the rind and squeeze the juice from the 2 lemons.
Place in a pan with the cream and sugar.
Bring to the boil and simmer for 15/20 minutes.
Pour into individual dishes, and leave to set in the fridge.
Serve garnished with fresh fruit or a tuille biscuit.

Marmalade and Ricotta Baskets

250g ricotta cheese
200ml double cream
orange marmalade
brandy baskets

serves 10

JOANNE KERSWELL,
SEVEN BAR AND RESTAURANT,
COCKERMOUTH

Whip cream until just before it holds its own shape, add ricotta and whisk again until firm enough to spoon. Fold in 2/3 tablespoons of a quality orange marmalade. Spoon mixture into brandy baskets. Chill for 1 hour and serve.

 tip.....

Mascarpone cheese can be used here instead of ricotta which will give a sweeter smoother texture. However, I think the coarseness and slight bitterness of the ricotta gives a better contrast to the sweet marmalade.

Marmalade Ice Cream

200ml double cream
200ml milk
$\frac{1}{2}$ vanilla pod or a drop of
vanilla essence
4 egg yolks
120g caster sugar
rind of a small orange
Note: Best made the day
before you need it

OLIVE JACKSON, DESSERT CHEF
EDENHALL COUNTRY HOTEL &
RESTAURANT, PENRITH

Mix egg yolks and sugar, beat until the mixture is pale and light.
Put cream, milk and vanilla pod in a pan bring to the boil.
Pour cream and milk over the egg yolks.
Strain and put mixture in a jug in the fridge and leave overnight.
On the next day take the liquid and add 1 dessert spoon of
marmalade before placing into the ice cream machine and churn.

tip.....

*Delicious served with Carrs Breadmaker's
Citrus Bread and Butter Pudding (page 92).*

Orange & Grand Marnier Ice Cream

6 egg yolks
6oz caster sugar
$\frac{3}{4}$ pint of milk
$\frac{3}{4}$ pint cream
$\frac{1}{4}$ pint Grand Marnier
2 tbsp thick cut orange
marmalade

BARRY QUINION,
FARLAM HALL, BRAMPTON

Cream together the egg yolks and sugar in a bowl.
Boil the milk and add to the mixture, return to the pan and cook,
stirring continuously until the mix coats the back of a spoon.
Remove from the heat, add the cream, this will stop the custard
from cooking on or curdling. Add the Grand Marnier and marmalade to the custard, mix and refrigerate.
When cool churn in an ice cream machine.

tip.....

*This recipe is particularly good as it
does not freeze rock hard. Serve with
an orange and raspberry fruit salad.*

Orange and Cranberry Pudding

150g/5oz self raising flour
1 tsp baking powder
150g/5oz butter, softened, plus extra for greasing
150g/5oz soft light brown sugar
1 tbsp golden syrup
3 free range eggs
1 tbsp dried cranberries
1 orange, peeled and sliced into rounds

For the sauce:
100g/3^{1}2oz caster sugar
175ml/6fl oz water
1 tbsp orange marmalade
1 tbsp cranberry jelly from a jar
2 oranges, juice only

To serve:
double cream, whipped until stiff peaks form when the whisk is removed.

Pre heat the oven to 200C/400F/gas mark 6.

Sift the flour and baking powder together into a bowl.

In a separate bowl, beat the butter, sugar and syrup together. Add the eggs, one at a time, beating to incorporate well before adding the next egg. Add the egg mixture to the bowl of flour and whisk well for two minutes, or until pale and light. Add the dried cranberries and fold in gently.

For the sauce, place the sugar, water, marmalade, cranberry jelly and orange juice into a sauce pan and heat gently to dissolve the sugar and marmalade. Bring to the boil and simmer gently for 5/10 minutes to form a thick syrup.

Grease four ramekins and place a disk of greaseproof paper, cut to fit the ramekins, in the base of each. Spoon a little of the sauce into each ramekin, then sit a round of orange on top.

Add the pudding mixture to almost fill the ramekins. Cover each ramekin with aluminium foil and transfer to a deep roasting tray. Half fill the tray with boiling water to create a bain-marie and transfer to the oven to bake for 20 minutes, or until the puddings have set.

To serve, turn out the puddings onto plates and serve with a dollop of whipped cream.

BY KIND PERMISSION OF SIMON RIMMER, TV CHEF, GREENS AT WEST DIDSBURY - SENT IN BY ANGELA WALTON, MOTHERBY

Striped Orange Jellies

1 pint of red jelly, a homemade raspberry or strawberry jelly would be best
1 pint of white blancmange flavoured with a tablespoon of rosewater
8 satsumas

IVAN DAY - FOOD HISTORIAN
www.historicfood.com

Cut a round about the size of a one pence piece from the top of each satsuma. Massage the skin of each fruit to loosen it from the flesh inside. Remove each segment with the end of a teaspoon until you have an empty skin. Use the satsuma pulp and juice for something else.

Put the satsuma skins on a large plate or tray in the refrigerator to cool. Pour about 4 teaspoons of cool, but liquid blancmange into each orange. Allow this first layer to set and then pour in a similar layer of red jelly. Repeat until the satsuma skins are full. When fully set, cut from top to bottom into quarters with a sharp knife and serve. Originally, these were garnished with myrtle leaves.

Everyone will be puzzled how you made these beautiful little striped jellies. Children love them. The great French chef Antonin Carême invented this recipe in the early 19th century.

Polenta in Orange Sauce

540ml milk
250ml water
142ml single cream
100g caster sugar
seeds of a vanilla pod (or a dash of good vanilla essence)
110g polenta
4 tbsp fine cut marmalade
2 egg yolks

serves 4

Whisk together 250ml milk, 250ml water, 50g caster sugar, the seeds from a vanilla pod (or dash of vanilla essence) and 110g polenta in a thick sauce pan and bring to the boil, stirring continuously.

When the polenta is bubbling hot and coming away from the pan, remove from the heat and put to one side.

Put $\frac{1}{4}$ pint of milk, $\frac{1}{4}$ pint of single cream and 4 tablespoons of good quality fine cut marmalade on to boil.

When the mixture starts boiling, remove from the heat.

Whisk two large egg yolks and 50g caster sugar till pale yellow, then add the cream mix in a steady stream, whisking while doing so. When mixed, place back into the pan and bring slowly back to the heat, but do not boil. Stir continuously until the sauce thickens and coats the back of the wooden spoon.

Remove the sauce from the heat and leave to one side. Put the grill on to pre heat. Shape the polenta into quenelles (rugby ball shapes) using two tablespoons and place 2/3 per serving into small oven proof serving dishes.

Mask with the orange custard, sprinkle with a little caster sugar (and grated orange zest if you like) and brown under the hot grill until glazed. Garnish with a sprig of fresh mint and serve with a nice glass of orange liqueur.

JIM BATY, CASA ROMANA
RESTAURANT, CARLISLE

This dish is delightfully different yet the warm polenta brings back fond memories of sweet semolina pudding.

Toasted Coconut Ice Cream
with hot brandy and orange mincemeat sauce

4 eggs, separated
4oz icing sugar, sieved
$\frac{1}{2}$ pint double cream, whipped
3 rounded tablespoons
desiccated coconut, toasted
until golden brown then
cooled.

For the sauce:
8oz mincement
grated rind of 1 orange
3 tablespoons brandy

serves 8

Whisk the egg whites until they are quite stiff then add the sieved icing sugar, spoonful by spoonful, whisking all the time.

In a separate bowl beat the yolks until smooth then fold them into the whipped cream. Fold the cream and yolk mixture into the egg white mixture, alternately with the cooled, toasted coconut.

Put the ice cream mixture into a polythene container with a lid and freeze. You do not need to beat this ice cream as it freezes but take it out of the deep freeze 20 minutes before you want to eat it.

To make the sauce put all the ingredients together in a saucepan and stir over a gentle heat. Don't let it boil.

Serve the sauce hot with the ice cream.

LADY CLAIRE MACDONALD, KINLOCH LODGE, ISLE OF SKYE
www.claire-macdonald.com

Caramelised Oranges

6 organic oranges
6oz organic sugar

Peel 4 oranges very carefully so that not one scrap of pith is left on them. Prepare a syrup heating the sugar with a teacupful of water until it is thick. Dip the oranges into the syrup turning them over so that the whole orange is well coated with the sugar. Leave them in the syrup for 2 minutes. Take them out and arrange them on a large dish.

Cut the peel very thinly from the other two oranges. Cut the peel into fine strips matchstick length. Plunge these into boiling water and cook for about 7 minutes to rid the peel of the bitter taste. Drain, then cook these in the syrup until the strips have begun to take on a transparent look and are becoming caramelised. Be careful this does not turn to toffee.

Place a spoonful of this caramelised peel on top of each orange. Serve very cold.

ANNETTE GIBBONS, COOKERY
PRESENTER AND PATRON -
HOSPICE AT HOME, CARLISLE
AND NORTH LAKELAND
www.cumbriaonaplate.co.uk

Lemon and Pistachio Nut Tart

Lemon pastry:
250g plain flour, sieved
60g caster sugar
125g unsalted butter
finely grated rind of one lemon
2 egg yolks

Filling:
350g ricotta cheese
90g caster sugar
3 eggs
finely grated rind of 1 lemon
and juice,
90g toasted chopped pistachio
nuts

serves 8

To make the pastry place all dry ingredients in a bowl.
Add softened butter, rind and yolks and mix until a smooth dough forms. Wrap in cling film and chill for 20 minutes.

To make the filling beat ricotta and sugar together. Add the eggs, lemon rind, juice and 80g of the nuts. Mix together until evenly combined.
Pre heat oven to 180C/gas 4.
Line a 20cm fluted, loose bottomed tin with the rolled out pastry, trim away the edges. Pour in the filling and smooth.
Top with the remaining chopped nuts.
Bake for about 1 hour or until golden and set.
Leave to cool in the tin and serve at room temperature, or chilled.

COLIN & LOUISA LeVOI,
QUINCE AND MEDLAR RESTAURANT, COCKERMOUTH

Lime Mousse

4oz butter
5 eggs
7oz caster sugar
5/6 limes
15fl oz double cream
summer berries

BARBARA KIRKWOOD,
BEREAVEMENT SUPPORT
CO-ORDINATOR,
HOSPICE AT HOME, CARLISLE
AND NORTH LAKELAND

Place the butter in a bowl and melt over a pan of gently simmering water. Using an electric whisk, beat the eggs/sugar until pale and mousse like and doubled in volume.
Add the butter and continue whisking over a gentle heat until the mixture thickens and leaves a trail on itself for 2/3 seconds (this will take about 20 minutes).
Remove from the heat and stir in the grated rind of the limes and 6 floz juice. Cool. Whisk cream until it holds its shape and fold into the lime juice mixture.
Pour into a freezer proof serving dish and freeze for at least 6 hours, preferably overnight.
Allow mousse to stand at room temperature for 5 minutes before serving with the berries. Spoon berries over the mousse if wished.

Sweet Lemon Rice

110g/4oz long grain rice, semi-cooked
85g/3oz double cream
30ml/1floz milk
3 tbsp caster sugar
1 orange, zest only
1 lemon, zest only

Caramelised oranges:
2 tbsp caster sugar
2 oranges, peeled and halved

serves 2

NICK MARTIN,
www.nickofthyme.co.uk

Place semi-cooked long grain rice into a saucepan with the double cream, milk and caster sugar.
Bring to a simmer and cook for 3/4 minutes.
Add the orange and lemon zest and continue cooking for 2/3 minutes.
For the caramelised oranges, heat the caster sugar in a small frying pan until it begins to caramelise. Add the orange halves. Toss to coat and cook for a further minute.
Serve the sweet lemon rice in a bowl with the caramelised oranges on top to garnish.

White Chocolate, Lemon and Thyme Mousse

250g milk
$\frac{1}{2}$ vanilla pod
50g egg yolk
50g caster sugar
25g plain flour
2 gelatine leaves, soaked
275g white chocolate
250g whipped cream
1 lemon, zest
1 lemon, juice
4 thyme sprigs, chopped

serves 6

Boil milk, vanilla and thyme.
Whisk egg and sugar,
beat in flour. Liaise with milk.
Return and simmer with lemon
for 4/5 mins. Add gelatine, add
chocolate, beat. Cool rapidly,
pass through sieve.
Fold in cream.

 tip.....

*Can also be spread between
leaves of chocolate or layers
of puff pastry.*

JOHN BADLEY, EXECUTIVE
HEAD CHEF, MACDONALD
LEEMING HOUSE

Orange and Lemon Essence (page 86)

Cakes, Bakes & Breads

Fruity Teabread (page 79)

Coconut Lime and Macadamia Cake

200g/7oz macadamia nuts
40g/1½oz self-raising flour
pinch of salt
6 eggs separated
165g/5¾oz sugar
1 lime (zest only), finely grated
45g/1½oz desiccated coconut

For the lime icing:
125g/4½oz icing
sugar, sifted
2 tbsp lime juice
1 tsp lime zest finely grated

Preheat the oven to 180C/350F, gas mark 4.
Place the nuts, flour and salt in the bowl of a food processor and process until the nuts are ground.
Place the egg yolks and sugar in a separate bowl and beat for three minutes, or until the mixture is pale and creamy. Fold through the zest and coconut, then the nut mixture.
Place the egg whites in a clean, dry, stainless steel bowl and whisk until stiff peaks form. Using a large metal spoon, fold lightly through the nut batter.
Spread the batter evenly into a 23cm (9in) greased or non-stick spring form cake tin. Bake for 40 minutes, or until the cake is lightly golden.
Meanwhile, make the icing. Combine all the icing ingredients in a bowl and mix until smooth and glossy.
Remove from the oven and leave to sit for 10 minutes in the tin. Turn the cake out onto a serving plate. Spread the lime icing over the warm cake, allowing it to drizzle down the sides.

NICK MARTIN, www.nickofthyme.co.uk

Fruity Teabread

2oz sultanas
2oz raisins
2oz dried figs, chopped
2oz dried apricots, chopped
½ pint hibiscus tea
4oz muscovada sugar
1 tbsp Seville orange
marmalade
½ tsp ground cinnamon
1 egg, beaten
8oz Watermill 85% self raising flour.
makes 1lb loaf

Grease and line a 1lb loaf tin.
Place the dried fruit in a bowl and pour over the hibiscus tea. Leave to soak for several hours or overnight.
Place remaining ingredients in another bowl. Drain the fruit reserving the liquid. Add the fruit to the other ingredients and stir, adding enough of the reserved liquid to make a soft mixture. When thoroughly combined spoon into a tin.
Bake at 150C for 1/1¼ hours, until the cake feels firm when pressed lightly.

THE WATERMILL, LITTLE SALKELD

Hay Close Citrus Drizzle

200g butter
250g sieved self raising flour
2 tsp baking powder
250g sugar
4 eggs
12 tbsp milk
zest of 2 large lemons
zest of 1 lime

Topping:
6 tbsp lemon juice
200g sugar

Heat oven to 180C.
Line and grease a tin 30 x 25 cm.
Put all ingredients into a large bowl.
Beat for 2/3 minutes until mixture drops off spoon (I use an electric mixer!)
Put in the tin and bake for 30/40 minutes.
Put the topping over whilst still hot.

ALISON FIELD, HAY CLOSE MAIZE MAZE, CALTHWAITE

Gluten Free Orange Cake

1 large orange, halved and pips removed
3 eggs,
8oz caster sugar
9oz ground almonds
$\frac{1}{2}$ tsp gluten-free baking powder

Purée the orange in a food processor. Whisk the eggs and sugar until thick and pale. Fold in almonds, baking powder and fruit puree. Pour into a lined 8 inch cake tin, and bake at 190C or 375F, gas mark 5 for about 45 minutes until firm and golden. When cool, dust with icing sugar.

JUNE SIMPSON, GREYSTOKE

Lemon Drizzle Cake

6oz margarine
6oz caster sugar
3 eggs
grated rind of 1 lemon
8oz self raising flour
pinch salt
2 tbsp milk

Topping:
4oz granulated sugar
juice of 2 lemons
grated rind of 1 lemon.

Cream margarine, sugar and grated rind of one lemon together. Beat in eggs and flour alternately, adding milk to make a soft consistency.
Put in prepared 8 inch cake tin (greased and bottom lined). Bake 160C or 350F, gas mark 3 for $1\frac{1}{4}/1\frac{1}{2}$ hours (checking after $1\frac{1}{4}$ hours).
While cooking, prepare topping by putting 4oz granulated sugar into basin with juice of 2 lemons and grated rind of 1 lemon and stir. When cake is cooked and still hot in tin, prod holes with a skewer all over the top of cake. Gently spoon topping over so that it soaks into top of cake.
Do not remove from tin until cold.

ELIZABETH PEACE, HESKET NEWMARKET. RECIPE FROM HAVEN GREEN BAPTIST CHURCH COOKERY BOOK 1977

My father attended Haven Green church in London for 60 years and this recipe - taken from the church cookery book - became a family favourite. He came to live with me in 1999 and enjoyed our 5 acre garden which is home to a family of red squirrels. They quickly became his friends. Towards the end of his life Hospice at Home enabled him to die peacefully in natural surroundings. Now, when people visit our garden, which we open to raise funds for Hospice at Home, we include tea and Lemon Drizzle Cake. We were so thrilled when the garden was featured in *Cumbria Life* magazine in August 2005.

The citrus lemons are like the sharp reality of dying but the process is sweetened by the ability to do so with dignity in one's own home through the care of Hospice at Home. **Elizabeth Peace**

Iced Marmalade Ginger Cake

8oz/250g margarine
8oz/250g caster sugar
8oz/250g marmalade
½ pt/300ml milk
11oz/325g plain flour
2oz/50g rolled oats
2 tsp bicarbonate of soda
1 tbsp ground ginger
¼ tsp grated nutmeg
2 eggs, beaten
2oz/50g chopped stem ginger
2oz/50g raisins

Icing:
3oz/75g soft butter
2oz/50g cream cheese
1oz/25g marmalade
grated zest of ½ orange
6oz/150g icing sugar

Place the margarine, sugar, marmalade and milk into a saucepan. Heat gently until the margarine has melted and the sugar has dissolved. Allow to cool slightly.

Sieve the flour into a large bowl, add the rolled oats, ground ginger, ground nutmeg and bicarbonate of soda and mix well.

Pour in the marmalade mixture from the pan, stirring all the time until a smooth batter forms.

Beat the eggs in a bowl, then using a fork stir in the chopped ginger and the raisins, now add this to the cake mixture and combine well. Pour the cake mixture into a lined tin.

Bake in a pre-heated oven of 160C/350F/gas mark 3 for 50/60 minutes. Allow the cake to cool completely in the tin before covering with the icing.

Combine the butter, cream cheese, marmalade and zest together using an electric whisk.

Gradually incorporate the sifted icing sugar. Using a spatula, spread over the top of the cool cake.

Store in an airtight tin.

JOAN GATE & MARGARET BROUGH, FOOD AND COMPANY
HESKET NEWMARKET www.foodandcompany.co.uk

Mary's Christmas Cake

1lb 6oz currants
8oz both sultanas & raisins
6oz cherries,
12oz butter
12oz soft brown sugar
4oz peel,
12oz plain flour
½ tsp cinnamon
1 tsp ground ginger
½ tsp mace (nutmeg)
6 eggs, 2 tbsp brandy/rum
lemon juice and rind.

Beat sugar and butter, add eggs, then flour, fruit and spices. Pour into a well lined 7 inch tin and cook at 120C/130C for 4/5 hours. Turn heat slightly lower after second hour.
Don't open oven door until cake is cooked.

MARY HILTON, BECKERMET WI

Jane's Breakfast Bread

1 tsp fast action easy bake yeast
15oz strong white flour
4 tbsp bran
1 tbsp golden caster sugar
1 tbsp extra virgin olive oil
1½ tbsp skimmed milk powder
1 tbsp cooking salt
1 tbsp ground cinnamon
310ml water
grated zest of 1 orange
5 ready to eat figs
6 ready to eat stoned prunes
6 ready to eat dried apricots
2 tbsp golden linseeds
2 tbsp pumpkin seeds

Place all ingredients in breadmaker, in order, up to water in the bread pan.

Set to raisin bake for a medium sized loaf and press start.

Chip figs, prunes and apricots into 2cm pieces and add, together with linseeds, pumpkin seeds and orange zest at the raisin beep. Leave now to complete cooking cycle.

Bread is good sliced and buttered, also good toasted with banana squashed on top.

JANE de LOOZE, KILMARNOCK

Please note all ingredients, quantities and instructions are designed for the Panasonic SD-206 Breadmaker. Amounts and method may need to be altered for other makes and models of breadmaker.

Lemon Biscoti

500g plain flour
500g caster sugar
5 eggs
1 tbsp baking powder
100g sultanas, sliced apricots, dates, pistachios, almonds, zest of 2 lemons

Mix together all ingredients, line on baking tray, approximately 2cm thick. Bake in the oven at 180C for 20/30 minutes
Then bake in the oven at 140C for 30/40 minutes until hard.

JOHN BADLEY, EXECUTIVE HEAD CHEF, MacDONALD LEEMING HOUSE

tip.....

These are good with mascarpone and fruit.

Lemon Muffins

2 lemons
1 tsp nutmeg
2 eggs
1 cup sugar
$\frac{1}{2}$ cup of oil
2 cups plain flour
1 cup yoghurt
1 tsp bicarbonate of soda

Zest lemons.
Add all ingredients (except juice from lemons) to zest and mix well.
Put into 9 large muffin cases.
Bake at 180C for 30/35 minutes.
Put juice of lemons into small bowl with 1 tablespoon full of sugar and stir.
Put this mix on top of the hot muffins.

THE VILLAGE BAKERY, MELMERBY

Lemon Slice

175g plain flour
125g butter
250g granulated sugar
2 tbsp plain flour
$\frac{1}{2}$ tsp baking powder
2 eggs
juice and rind of 1 lemon
icing sugar (to decorate)

Heat oven to 170C/325F, gas mark 3.
Oil and line a 20.5cm/8 inch square cake tin with bakewell paper.
Rub together 175g flour with butter and 50g sugar to form a stiff shortbread. Press into prepared tin.
Bake for 20 minutes until pale golden.
In a bowl or processor mix 200g sugar, 2 tablespoons plain flour and baking powder, eggs and lemon.
Pour over the cooked base.
Bake for 20 minutes, it should be nearly set but a bit wobbly in the centre!
Dust with icing sugar and cut into squares.

CLAIRE EASTON, THE OLD SAWMILL TEAROOM,
MIREHOUSE, KESWICK

Lemon Muffins (page 84)

Orange and Lemon Essence

3 oranges or 3 lemons
vodka

 tip.....

One spoonful of this mixture is sufficient to flavour a large cake.

Peel the oranges or lemons very thinly, avoiding any pith.
Pack the peel in a small glass preserving jar and press down forcefully.
Cover with vodka and secure lid firmly.
Shake vigorously every day for six weeks.

SIR JOHN SCOTT - THE COUNTRYMAN

Rosemary and Lemon Cake

3 tbsp zest and juice from 1 unwaxed lemon
1 level tbsp finely chopped rosemary
225g/8oz unsalted butter softened
175g/6oz light caster sugar
3 free range eggs beaten

350g/12oz plain flour
2 level tsp baking powder
1/2 tbsp milk (or buttermilk)
1 level tbsp caster sugar

Prepare a 2lb (900g) loaf tin.
Preheat the oven to 170C/325F, gas mark 3
Place the softened butter, sugar, lemon zest and rosemary in a mixing bowl and whisk until light and fluffy. Gradually whisk in the beaten eggs, adding a little of the flour if the mixture looks as if it might curdle.
Fold in the rest of the sifted flour and baking powder and a pinch of salt. Stir in the lemon juice. The mixture should have a soft dropping consistency. If it is a bit stiff stir in a tablespoon or so of milk. Place the mix into the prepared loaf tin, level the surface and sprinkle with the caster sugar. Bake in the preheated oven for one hour. The cake may take a little longer to cook, depending on the oven. Test with a clean skewer that it comes out clean. Cool in the tin for 10 minutes before turning out and cool completely on a wire rack. Wrap in foil to keep the cake.

ANNETTE GIBBONS, COOKERY PRESENTER, PATRON - HOSPICE AT HOME, CARLISLE AND NORTH LAKELAND
www.cumbriaonaplate.co.uk

─CARRS
BREADMAKER

is delighted to sponsor this unique cookbook packed with mouth-watering dishes. In this section we have included four recipes of our own which show off the culinary versatility of flour and bread. Visit our website www.carrsbreadmaker.info for further information and more fabulous recipes.

Citrus Bread and Butter Pudding (page 92)

Stilton & Marmalade Bread

a recipe from

CARRS
BREADMAKER

250g Carrs Breadmaker Strong White Flour
250g Carrs Breadmaker Strong Brown Flour
1 tbsp butter
2 tbsp milk powder
1 tsp salt
2 tbsp thick cut Seville orange marmalade
100g white Stilton, crumbled
1 tsp fast action dried yeast
325ml water

By bread machine

Follow the manufacturers' instructions regarding the order of liquid/dry ingredients, and set your machine to the normal/basic setting, large loaf, medium crust.

By hand

Put the flour into a large bowl, add the butter and rub in with the fingertips until the mixture resembles fine breadcrumbs. Add the milk powder, salt, marmalade, cheese and yeast. Gradually mix in warm water to make a soft dough.

Knead well on a lightly floured surface for about 10 minutes until smooth and elastic then place it back in the bowl, cover loosely with lightly oiled plastic wrap. Leave the dough in a warm place for about an hour to rise.

Tip the dough out onto a lightly floured surface, knead well, place in a greased $1\frac{1}{2}$lb loaf tin and cover loosely with lightly oiled plastic wrap. Leave the dough in a warm place for about half an hour.

Remove plastic wrap, sprinkle with flour and bake in a preheated oven 200C (400F), gas mark 6 for 30/40 minutes.

Orange and Poppy Seed Rolls

a recipe from
CARRS BREADMAKER

250g Carrs Breadmaker Strong White Flour
2 tbsp butter
2 tbsp milk powder
1 tsp salt
3 tbsp poppy seeds
1 orange, grated rind and juice
1¼ tsp fast action dried yeast
2 tbsp honey
275ml water

Glaze: 1 egg yolk and 1 tbsp water

Follow the manufacturers' instructions regarding the order of liquid/dry ingredients, and set your machine to the dough setting. Tip the dough out onto a lightly floured surface, knead well and cut into 20 pieces. Shape each into a small ball and arrange, spaced well apart on a greased baking sheet. Cover loosely with oiled cling film and leave to rise in a warm place for 30 minutes. Remove cling film, brush with glaze and bake at 200C (400F, gas mark 6) for 12/15 minutes.

Pissaladière

a recipe from
CARRS BREADMAKER

250g Carrs Breadmaker Strong White Flour
$\frac{1}{2}$ tsp salt
1 tsp caster sugar
$\frac{3}{4}$ tsp fast action dried yeast
4 tsp lemon and dill infused olive oil
150ml water
Topping:
500g onion, thinly sliced and 3 cloves of garlic crushed, lightly fried in 3 tbsp olive oil and 1 tsp caster sugar until softened
few stems of fresh lemon thyme
50g anchovy fillets, drained and halved lengthways
75g pitted black olives
freshly ground black pepper

Follow the manufacturers' instructions regarding the order of liquid/dry ingredients, and set your machine to the dough setting. Tip the dough out onto a lightly floured surface, knead well. Roll out to a rectangle then press into a greased 25 x 37cm shallow baking tin, until the dough reaches the edges.

Spoon onion/garlic mix onto base in an even layer leaving a narrow border of dough at edges. Strip leaves from lemon thyme and sprinkle over topping. Make a lattice pattern over the onions with the halved anchovy fillets and fill in each hole with an olive. Season with pepper. Leave in a warm place for 30 minutes. Bake in a preheated oven at 220C (425F, gas mark 7) for 12/15 minutes.

Citrus Bread and Butter Pudding

a recipe from
——CARRS BREADMAKER

6 slices crusty white bread
(made with Carrs
Breadmaker flour of course)
50g butter
75g currants
40g soft light brown sugar
600ml milk
2 eggs
grated zest of 1 orange
and 1 lemon

Spread the bread with the butter and cut the slices into quarters. Arrange half in a greased ovenproof dish. Sprinkle with $\frac{3}{4}$ of the currants and half the sugar. Top with the remaining bread, butter-side up and sprinkle over the remaining sugar.

Beat together the milk, eggs, most of the orange and lemon zest and pour over the bread and allow to stand for 30 minutes.

Preheat the oven to 160C (325F, gas mark 3) Bake pudding in the oven for 45/60 minutes until set and golden.

Sprinkle with the remaining currants and grated zest and serve.

Useful Tips

Orange Fire Lighter

In this day of recycling how clever to have a use for your orange peel after making, for example, orange juice.
Just pop used orange halves in a meat tin in the bottom oven of your Aga overnight and next day you can use them as firelighters. Not only do these smell lovely but they look pretty in the fire place before the fire is lit.

YVONNE MARPLES, ORTON

About Citrus Essential Oils

We all respond to that tingling, zingy, zesty feeling that you get when you smell or eat citrus fruit. Our senses activate and sensations of being refreshed and uplifted are the beneficial effects of citrus oils, being antiseptic, stimulating and tonic. Many commercial products contain citrus oils from washing up liquid, food, teas to cosmetic products.

When using essential oils care should be taken as citrus oils require careful consideration due to their potential to oxidise and degrade. They have a short shelf life of 6 months and should be kept in cool conditions. Degraded oils increase their acid content and the precious active aldehydes diminish and so the oil is tainted and should not be used.

Citrus oils are derived from the Rutaceae family and obtained from 3 different sites in the plant:
Peel : Bergamot, grapefruit, lemon, mandarin and orange.
Leaf : Petitgrain oils, mainly from bitter orange but occasionally from other citrus trees.
Flower : Neroli mainly from the bitter orange tree for therapeutic purposes.

Citrus oils may cause skin irritation and are phototoxic (increasing sensitivity to sunlight) and even with commercially sourced products one must be aware of this and care taken not to apply body lotions etc. containing citrus if known to have a sensitive skin or intending sun exposure within 6 hours. Also particular oils have contraindications with certain prescribed medications and medical conditions therefore advice from a qualified Aromatherapist should always be consulted.

However citrus oils do have so many valuation effects: antibacterial, antifungal, calming, balancing (calming, energising to the nervous system) to name just a few and through individual selection the best outcome can be uniquely yours.

A general note on the use of all essential oils: must not be applied directly to the skin but must always be diluted in a carrier oil (such as grapeseed oil). Over the past years research has suggested that low concentration of oils still have beneficial effect i.e. 10ml carrier with 1 drop essential oil.

Care should always be taken with contact of essential oils and clothing, furnishings and polished surfaces as staining can occur.

Citrus fruits are so evident in our daily life in the shampoo, shower gel we use, cleaning materials around the house and in our diet.

JUDY GOPSILL
COMPLEMENTARY THERAPIST
HOSPICE AT HOME,
CARLISLE & LAKELAND

Index